The Full Ripened Grain

A Memoir of Healing and Hope

By
Benay Nordby

Benay Nordby

© 2013 by Benay Nordby

This book is dedicated to my mother, Wanda Florene Willingham, and my father, Blake Hudson, whose legacy is love. And to my husband Lynn, and my children Evan, Eden, and Kirk, who share it.

Table of Contents

Introduction 1

A Pumpkin in December 3

A Pebble in My Shoe... 10

How Can I Keep from Singing? 20

Home is Where The Hurt is 27

Graduation USA 46

Dateline Enumclaw... 51

Missing Mom... 74

Mother Moments 84

Beverly's Gift 91

Eating Grief 100

Practical Matters 106

Waking from The American Dream 112

Mom's Farewell.. 126

March Reruns 134

The Full Ripened Grain

The Tuna Rebellion 144

Changes 151

An Anniversary in May 160

Ghosts of Snowater.. 167

Acknowledgements 174

When I have fears that I may cease to be
before my pen has gleaned my teeming brain;
before high piled books, in charactry,
hold like rich garners the full ripened grain...

– John Keats

INTRODUCTION

Everyone has a colorful life. You just have to get out your crayons.

I began this project well into my second half of life, the day I arranged a collection of my journals on the top of my bed. Gazing at the collection, I marveled at the materials, colors, and sizes of the books spread before me. They were leather, paper, and fabric-covered receptacles of life planned and life altered, love made and love betrayed. The pattern of the plaid bedspread divided book from book, year from year. Some of the journals were gifts I had filled with dreams and teenaged angst. I chose the others as sturdy keepers of personal truths: simple, daily truths and complex, life-altering acceptance of human truths and God's truths. Inside them were handwritten accounts of events in my life and the lives of my father, mother, sisters, husband, and children. I used

The Full Ripened Grain

information imparted by my parents, in confidence, as the basis for descriptions of events prior to my birth and of my early childhood.

Because I was the "baby" of the family, my sisters filled me in later in life about many aspects of our parents' lives. Also because I was the youngest, I thought I had weathered our private storm of social issues and life decisions more successfully than my sisters. That was not true.

From childhood friends, I learned that my family seemed to have something special: personality, talent, humor, leadership, wit, and savvy. My own share of these traits blossomed in school, work, marriage, motherhood, community service, and a maturing religious faith. My Baby Boomer friends and I thought we could have it all and reached for it. At midlife, I faltered, feeling mentally ill with no explanation as to why my otherwise idyllic life had produced such utter sadness. I was compelled to look for answers.

"A graceful hand," my Aunt Faye used to say about my penmanship. But graceful recollections? No. They were grace filled.

Although the journals were written chronologically, I decided I had a story to tell that was not chronological. Connecting past to present seemed the only way to write it.

I got out my crayons and began.

How long, O Lord? Will you forget me forever?
How long will you hide your face from me?
How long must I wrestle with my thoughts
And every day have sorrow in my heart?
How long will my enemy triumph over me?

Look on me and answer, O Lord my God.
Give light to my eyes, or I will sleep in death;
My enemy will say, "I have overcome him,"
And my foes will rejoice when I fall.

But I trust in your unfailing love;
My heart rejoices in your salvation.
I will sing to the Lord,
For he has been good to me.

– Psalm 13

A PUMPKIN IN DECEMBER

Pumpkins have always been on the A-list of autumn for me. In late August, the vines unfurl in the Pacific Northwest, promising plans for September with the ripening squashes and the weatherman's cliché "the frost is on the pumpkin."

The Full Ripened Grain

By October, the markets in our town are bricked in by walls of orange pumpkins. It is a cheerful sight. There are petite sugar pumpkins piled high, while the mammoth ones stand ready for Halloween mayhem. I always buy a couple, one for a table centerpiece and a big one for the front porch. Kept cool and unmarred, they last in harmony with the season until Thanksgiving Day.

But the season changes abruptly. Colors clash. The pumpkin that sat center stage looks out of place with the glitzy red ribbons of December. Finally relocated to the rain-soaked deck or the back of the refrigerator, it waits in exile. There is nothing sadder than a pumpkin in December.

When my own sense of harmony began to clash with my surroundings in midlife, I entered a time of personal exile. Maybe what happened to me was predictable. Maybe it was the agonizing twenty-year vigil I kept while my mother lay in a vegetative state, the victim of medical malpractice. Maybe it was the long-delayed diagnosis of lifelong Tourette syndrome tics. Maybe it was the unacknowledged anger and childhood grief withheld over my parents' divorce and my father's secret life. Maybe it was the unexpected pregnancy in my late thirties and a postpartum hormone problem. Maybe it was living in a fishbowl in a small city and the high expectations of church and community. Maybe it was the pressure of responsibility serving as the trustee of a college while taking care of the needs of husband, home and three young children. As a new century approached with all its hopefulness, I became sadder than a pumpkin in December.

Depression assaulted me and spoiled my joy. It took me away emotionally from the things that gave life its sweetness. As much as my family and community asked of me—demanded of me—I pulled away harder and harder, resenting every effort I felt forced to make. I was filled with anger and anguish and sadness. Anger at God for what was happening to me and anguish that I could not seem to snap out of it. I knew my life was filled with many good things. Why was I so sad?

I thought that these feelings would go away if I had enough faith. I prayed meekly for help, then raised my furious fist to God, trudging the two blocks to our Lutheran church, on call for yet another committee meeting in His service.

A vague perception of personal slights—real and imagined—fueled emotional ammunition against the well-meaning people around me. While I was standing at the sink washing dishes, my rage would boil over in an imagined argument. I felt as if I were trapped underwater, kicking upward with all my strength. Occasionally, I would surface with enough breath to call out for help.

I signed up for an exercise class. It was one of a long line of popular aerobic dance classes I tried, filled with young women staving off the effects of childbirth and approaching age milestones, whether thirty or forty. My toddler went to the nursery willingly, making it easy on me. But my overweight

The Full Ripened Grain

figure in the mirror disappointed me despite the strenuous aerobics. On my hands and knees, lifting my legs alternately, stretching and pulling muscles, my tears dropped to the floor. A church friend was in the class so one day I invited her over to my home, just ten minutes away. Rushing home, I straightened up the kitchen, made fresh coffee, and got my son ready for his nap. What a pleasure it was, looking forward to company and girl talk without baby interruptions. But more than an hour passed before she finally arrived. She had seen a mutual friend downtown and had coffee at the bakery. I was puzzled and my feelings were hurt. Hadn't I made myself clear? Why didn't she say she was invited to my house? Both of them were welcome. But they didn't come. I fumed inwardly like a fourth grader whose best friend had chosen to play with someone else at recess. My baby son woke up and cried.

With hindsight, the symptoms seem clear. But at the time, I was unable to recognize the symptoms of depression. Today, television commercials list the symptoms while advertising medications. For many people, these meds bring normalcy and joy back to their lives.

But in the midst of my depression and my ignorance, I reeled with the daily struggle just to keep up with the laundry and feed my family. In reality, these times were filled with endearing moments, but I was hardly aware enough to notice them. My healthy baby boy grinned at me and

A Pumpkin in December

compelled me to smile back, compelled me to get out of bed to care for him and his older brother and sister. Even our pet beagle tried her best to comfort me, staying close. But I usually interpreted that as being "constantly underfoot."

The holiday season became a nightmare of pressure to buy, perform, serve, decorate, cook, and clean, both at home and at church. I had hoped never to burden my children with a Scrooge-like mother. Could my children sense my dread?

Once, past the push to Christmas Eve, there was a blessed moment of peace. After a candlelight service, it was nearly midnight. I sang my solo upstairs in the choir loft and crept quietly downstairs and out the church door. I paused, knowing my husband, Lynn, was home wrapping gifts, having tucked in the children after an earlier service.

The big Norman oak doors of the church thudded softly behind me, muffling the sound of the last hymn. Alone in the clear winter night, I reveled in the moonlit shadows on the sparkling, snow-crusted steps. I felt peaceful. Reassured. I knew I would make it through the busy day to come. But as the year wound down, my feelings continued to spiral downward with it.

For weeks, there were hushed, desperate moments of conversation with my bewildered husband trying to understand my anxiety, my gloom, the feeling there was no future for me. Urgently, I explained how it felt as if I was standing with my nose pressed against a brick wall, unable to

The Full Ripened Grain

see over it or around it. Emotionally stranded, this dear man never blamed, never accused, never shamed, never criticized me. The vow to love me in sickness and in health was being sorely tested. At my most unlovable, I was still loved.

Lynn and I and the kids were gathered in our kitchen on a weekday evening when the phone rang. I answered it. It was our pastor calling, asking if I would sing soprano in a quartet for a church service. The date was nearing and it would require a couple of practices. Although I stayed calm on the phone, feelings welled inside me. I denied the feelings and obediently, I said yes. The moment I hung up the phone, I felt as if I had swallowed a bottle of emotional ipecac. With my family looking on, I screwed up my face and spat out a rage of tears and resentment. "I CANNOT DO ONE MORE THING!"

Almost immediately, the phone rang again. In a conditioned response, my befuddled husband walked to the phone and answered it. The kids were quiet, shocked by my outburst.

"It's for you," he said seriously, offering the receiver.

I stared at him in stunned disbelief. He expected me to take the call?

My hand lifted itself. It was the pastor again. The plans had been cancelled and we would do it another time. God had heard my lament.

I was so in need of help and didn't know where to find it. It was not at all a part of the culture of our

A Pumpkin in December

family to seek mental health counseling. The "airing of dirty linen" was not done in public and personal pain was merely absorbed. It was not a subject to share with strangers. References to "my shrink" and psychiatry were only in funny Woody Allen films or frightening movies about psychotic criminals. I did not want to be associated with either. But the culmination of life events was taking its toll. Finally, my husband said, "I want my wife back."

I went to look for her.

My presence will go with you, and I will give you rest.

– Exodus 33:14

A PEBBLE IN MY SHOE

When I found myself pregnant at 36, my lifelong nervous tics worsened. The expecting had been, well, unexpected. After sixteen years of marriage, successful birth control, and child spacing, I had an unplanned pregnancy. Frankly, I was a little embarrassed. I was by no means too old to have another child, but I had other plans in mind now that our son was eight and our daughter was four and almost ready for school. I had my boy and my girl and was thinking my family was finished and I might go back to work. I was shaken by the turn of events.

Apparently, the stress had exacerbated my tics. I was blissfully unaware of it, but others, who knew me well, watched and worried without bringing up the subject to me directly. On the eve of our new baby's birth, I dreaded my third C-section so much,

A Pebble in My Shoe

I just wasn't ready. Despite my misgivings, a healthy new son joined our crew. He was precious.

While I was teaching Vacation Bible School that summer, one of my fourth graders asked, "Mrs. Nordby, why do you shake your head and shrug your shoulder?" I did not know how to respond. I was not consciously aware of it. Feeling uncomfortable, I just told him the truth.

"I don't know."

Later that day, one of the mothers played a video of the morning's events. Stunned and staring, I watched myself as I had been caught candidly in the background. My head was shaking mildly to the right, almost constantly as if I were miming the answer "no." At the same time, my right shoulder shrugged forward, a slight jerk now and then.

I left the church in tears, horrified that something was seriously wrong with me. Was it a disease? A brain tumor? Why had nothing been said to me about this before? An innocent child had broached a subject my family had never mentioned to me.

The next morning I was on the phone to my OB/gyn, who knew my medical history best. I asked for a referral to a neurologist. He gave me the name of a doctor in Seattle and assured me this was most likely just a "nervous habit."

My first visit to the neurologist, Dr. Robert Agner, was an unconventional exam. I explained my symptoms on the phone to him and he asked some unusual questions. Did I ever have obsessive thoughts? Did I do things over and over again? The questions triggered some visions of myself that only I knew about. Occasionally, when drying my hair, my right arm might jerk upward, striking the bathroom cabinet. The re-reading of paragraphs kept me from making progress in a book. These episodes gave me anguish I never admitted to anyone. I just didn't talk about them, thinking it was too private and embarrassing.

When I arrived at my appointment, Dr. Agner emerged from behind the reception desk. Walking toward me with a gentle smile on his face, he took me by both hands and led me into a workroom just off the waiting area. He said he had a hunch about the symptoms I had described on the phone. He wanted to immediately watch the tics I had described. I didn't know what he expected or what to do. A short time later, a second doctor appeared. While Dr. Agner questioned me, this physician watched me and started taking notes.

"Have you been under any unusual stress lately?" he asked.

Hearing his question was like opening a water main. I started to speak timidly, then gushed.

"My mother has been in a persistent vegetative state for many years and last year I had an unexpected baby and moved into a bigger house and I live in a small town and have lots of obligations to our church and I have two other children who are wonderful and gifted but demand a lot of attention and I serve on the board of trustees of a college. It's a gubernatorial appointment." I took a breath and trembled.

Our talk was followed by a thorough physical exam. I was instructed to return in a week and bring my husband along. It sounded serious. We were quiet in the car on the return trip to the doctor's office. To our surprise, the doctor walked into the office with a pleasant expression.

"I have good news for you!" he said. "You have Tourette syndrome. Named for Georges Gilles de la Tourette. It is a neurological disorder."

He selected a thick book from his bookshelf. It was a massive volume outlining the history of the discovery and the symptoms of this rare disorder. Dr. Agner had not said "mental illness." He had said, "neurological disorder."

Something is wrong with my brain, I thought. This is good news?

As it turned out, the second doctor had identified several symptoms of the disorder expressed in my movements as I spoke. I seemed to incorporate them rather well into my gestures and personality, he noted.

I did?

So I didn't have a brain tumor. I didn't have multiple sclerosis or Parkinson's disease. The good news was that it was not life-threatening. I was "suffering" from a malady I had only heard of in relation to some people who grunt and bark and utter curse words uncontrollably. It turns out those cases are rare, but they are the visible tip of the

The Full Ripened Grain

iceberg. According to this doctor, thousands of people show mild tics all the time, with each body expressing its own "style."

Hearing his words was hardly a relief. He hastened to tell me Tourette syndrome is not degenerative and it does not affect intelligence. The physical tics usually wax and wane, but the symptoms will not worsen to a great degree. Its cause is unknown.

He told me about the Tourette Syndrome Association, which provides information and support. We talked about starting some medication. Then my husband and I left his office as if the diagnosis was nothing more than a cold requiring aspirin.

On the way home, Lynn tried to lighten the situation by referring to the support group.

"What do you suppose their national theme song is—'Twist and Shout'?"

It was years before I laughed at that.

***

I kept the diagnosis to myself, as if not talking about it could help me keep my secret for a little longer. I might as well have tried to keep a missing limb secret. The truth—which I could not acknowledge openly—was that I had been hounded by my own personal demon for a lifetime. It was with me in the first grade when I tilted my chair haphazardly and fell, crashing to the floor. My

A Pebble in My Shoe

teacher grabbed me off the floor, reminding how she had asked me not to do that. My six-year-old face is forever frozen in a grimace in my group class picture.

I read all I could find about Tourette syndrome. There happened to be a television talk show with TS as a subject. Self-consciously, I stared at the TV, realizing I was "one of them." I wrote a letter to the guest with TS. Somehow it seemed easier to talk to a stranger about this than a good friend. My memory whirled as I sifted out the incidents that had frightened me, for which I had no explanation. I started a file with newspaper clippings on the subject and newsletters from the Tourette Syndrome Association in New York. I needed to know as much as I could.

My return trips to the doctor started a trial of harsh medications that only added to my misery. I felt sleepy and slightly confused. I gained weight. I needed to be fast on my feet with a toddler at home. My tics slowed but so did my emotional barometer. Nothing was very funny or very sad. It was the ultimate feeling of apathy. Who needs an apathetic wife and mother? Ultimately, the best medicine was no medicine and some psychotherapy that helped me purge the bafflement I felt over this "outing" of my tics.

Hesitantly, I asked people about their impressions. From family members to the eye doctor, all confirmed they were aware of my shaking head and other tics.

The Full Ripened Grain

Hard as it was to hear, my sister Beverly was direct.

"I have never introduced you to anyone who did not ask me later if you have some sort of nervous problem," she said.

Ouch.

Gingerly, I asked others. Yes, they said. Why had no one ever mentioned it to me?

"We always thought it was just part of you!" was the standard answer.

To my husband I asked, "Do you mean that all these years, I have been singing solos in front of people while shaking?"

"Well, no. Your tics seem to disappear when you are singing," he said.

It proved to be true. A phenomenon of the disorder is that intense concentration on a task can temporarily stop the tics. In his book *An Anthropologist on Mars*, neurologist Dr. Oliver Sacks writes about a surgeon with TS whose tics subside during operations. My research revealed stories of concert pianists and sports figures who managed to live high profile lives with TS. It was rather fascinating.

I watched my children closely, so worried that the genetic component of the disorder would show itself in them. Boys have TS more often than girls. The classic onset of TS is between age six and fifteen. It is closely associated with obsessive compulsive disorder. Our gifted first son Evan was already eleven and showed only some obsession

A Pebble in My Shoe

with certain topics and a one-track mind that accompanied a tenacious personality. Our daughter Eden and second son Kirk remained healthy and showed no signs of any tics. I was so relieved!

It happened that Washington State's TSA support chapter had occasional meetings with seminars. After attending a few meetings, I just preferred to ignore my own situation as much as possible. The knowing still hurt. Then an article about a boy with TS who had written a letter of protest to the producers of the animated television series *The Simpsons* appeared in the *Seattle Times*. It seemed that Bart Simpson tried to convince his teacher he could not take a test due to a sudden case of Tourette syndrome. The local boy and his mother thought it was no laughing matter. It got media attention. I decided to add my two cents by sending a letter with a few other thoughts. I did not expect a reply.

It was one of those quiet nights with everyone watching television when the phone rang.

"Is this Mrs. Nordby?"

"Yes. Who's calling?"

"This is Mike Reiss, the producer of *The Simpsons*."

Whoa, man.

"I just had to call and tell you, your letter made my day."

A Hollywood producer read my letter! And liked my writing!

"Thank you!"

The Full Ripened Grain

"Yes, we passed the letter all around the office. Everyone read it."

Strangers in Hollywood who work on *The Simpsons* were reading my ideas!

"Well, I just thought the more people who know about TS, the better," I said. "Bart has many friends. Why not make one of them a kid with TS?"

"My favorite part is the thing your husband said about 'Twist and Shout.'"

I couldn't believe I was happy my husband had said that. It was good material.

We talked for twenty minutes and he ended the conversation promising to send our children some Simpson souvenirs. The package arrived a few days later. I began to feel a lot better about my TS.

The revelation about my Tourette syndrome tics and the accompanying angst became one reason for my depression. Like a death in the family, I had gone through the steps of grief over the loss of one self-image and the acceptance of a new one.

My next singing assignment was a duet in a church production of *Godspell*. The song is called "By My Side," and the words made no sense to me throughout the rehearsals. But on the morning of the performance, I awoke with light streaming through the blinds, and the words in my head. I sensed some insight about me and Tourette syndrome and God.

Where are you going?
Can you take me with you?

A Pebble in My Shoe

*Let me skip the road with you... I can dare
　myself...
I'll put a pebble in my shoe
And watch me walk
I shall call the pebble Dare
Dare shall be carried
And when we both have had enough
I will take him from my shoe, singing
Meet your new Road!
Then I'll take your hand, finally glad that
　you
are here by my side.*

The TS was just a pebble in my shoe, annoying me, distracting me and daring me to carry on down the road of life. Rather than blaming God, I decided to take Him along with me and show Him what I could do.

I will sing of mercy and justice;
To You, O Lord, I will sing praises

– Psalm 101:1

HOW CAN I KEEP FROM SINGING?

If you really want to get to know someone well, attend their funeral. It is a golden time to learn the value of someone's life and see a personal legacy displayed. That is, of course, if you are not a celebrity and a candidate for the A&E Biography series. The writers will dwell on public achievement and rarely give the audience a glimpse into the personal moments that nurture or destroy human beings.

On a recent autumn morning, the Catholic church in our small city was filled to the brim with people celebrating the life of a faithful old member. She was pretty famous by our community standards, having lived here forever, teaching piano to her children, her children's children, and everyone else's children. Sitting amid holy water droplets and the fragrance of incense, I listened as her grown grandchildren eulogized her tearfully.

How Can I Keep from Singing?

One granddaughter reminisced about her weekly piano lessons with her grandma. These lessons gave her the foundation for a college career of musical achievement. She expressed her gratitude for receiving a gift she could share with everyone. A grandson told the congregation, "The quality of music in heaven has just been raised a notch."

They described a beautiful legacy. No one said, "She could be a demanding pain in the butt."

It is at these rites of passage that we take account of those gifts entrusted to us and learn how they have been put to use.

I have been given a singing voice to share and I do that regularly at church and in community theater. The ability to sing was taken for granted in my family. Dad had a pleasant baritone. Mom's voice was solid—on pitch and a warm soprano. Each daughter could not only carry a tune competently but also put on a show at school or for family visitors. My father played the piano while we sang for any relatives or friends who would listen. It was mainstay Sunday afternoon entertainment reminiscent of our parents' southern upbringing where Baptist quartets harmonized to our father's piano music. We sang few songs in harmony, so our trio's rendition of "Blue Moon" was the foundation of our repertoire. Wintertime brought variety to cornered relatives as we sang a swingy "Winter Wonderland." Our "show" was pretty standard when expanded. Big sister Brenda jazz danced solo to Dad's version of "The

The Full Ripened Grain

Stripper," a surprising top-forty hit in 1962. Beverly was encouraged to tell a joke. I had my own solo, "May You Always," made famous by the McGuire Sisters.

Like most of Middle America, we watched the weekly Lawrence Welk Show on television. We seethed and felt ashamed of ourselves for not being the Lennon Sisters. Dad praised their sound, their hairdos, their dresses and smiles. Beverly looked a little like Peggy Lennon. Janet Lennon was my age. But there was no comparison, really.

"Sure, Dad," we whined, "we could look like that if we had hairdressers and wardrobe experts." But he didn't forgive us for not knowing how to become famous.

Our only training came from public schools where Miss Donna Keopke was the vocal teacher. She knew my sisters and me as she made rounds from school to school. From fourth grade chorus through high school concert choir, I sang a breadth of music from Broadway musicals to folk music to sacred Bach. Nowhere else did I learn what my voice could do, for my parents had never heard of singing lessons. None of us learned to play the piano, despite our obvious musicality. We just let Dad play for us.

I came to appreciate my voice as a special gift for meeting people and making new friends. I even met my future husband during rehearsals for a musical, *The Pajama Game*. Entering college, I auditioned for the top performance ensemble and

How Can I Keep from Singing?

made it. We traveled and performed on school breaks.

Five years later, in a new home in Washington State, I was in demand for solos, singing in the church choir and often at weddings and funerals. Home was within walking distance of both the church and the local funeral home. I was available on short notice. I learned it is easier to sing at a funeral than a wedding.

Weddings are booked far in advance. The family wants to know in January if you will be free in June. The bride would like to audition you if she hasn't had "the pleasure," which requires a meeting with an accompanist. She wants you to sing a romantic song made famous in an obscure movie and recorded by Melissa Manchester. The sheet music is always hard to find. She wants you to show up at the rehearsal on Friday night, thereby dispensing with the entire weekend's plans. When your best friends call to offer their gorgeous condominium free for the weekend, you breathe a sigh and say, "No, can't make it. Got a wedding."

It has always been very important to me to sing well and in the case of a wedding, the pressure is on. After all, this is the most important day in the lives of two people and someone is probably going to record the event. A froggy voice opening the ceremony might be permanently recorded for the bride and groom to remember. "Please God," I would pray, "No mistakes. Sing through me." He always did.

The Full Ripened Grain

Funerals don't have rehearsals. They happen on weekdays, usually. The family is grateful in a way that is so humbling. It reminds you of the blessing of having something you can do for this family in a time of grief. And let's face it, if you make a mistake in a song at a funeral, you haven't spoiled anyone's day.

I attended Trinity Lutheran Church in Enumclaw, Washington for eighteen years, singing my heart out up in the choir loft behind the congregation. At the time of a funeral, it felt a little like eavesdropping. Many funerals were for individuals I did not know personally. Nonetheless, each time I sang I felt rich with privilege, being there at the end of someone's life, listening to the warm stories and memories inspired by love and grief. Each is powerful.

A friend called to ask me to sing at her father's funeral. Mr. Sandberg had been a teacher for thirty years. As I sat in the rear of the chapel, I wondered if one could count the lives touched by a lifetime of teaching. But no counting is necessary. Just one story, a sweet surprise.

Toward the end of the service, a young woman stood up to say why she had come to honor her former teacher that day. As a girl, she had been teased cruelly by fellow students. She was on the verge of desperation, feeling persecuted. One day, Mr. Sandberg left the classroom momentarily and asked for good behavior while he was gone. The taunting began again. At that point, she recollected,

How Can I Keep from Singing?

her feelings erupted. Out of control and angry, she shoved her desk over, spilling its contents on the floor. What must have been an astonished classroom of students waited for Mr. Sandberg. She trembled. But when Mr. Sandberg returned to the classroom he took in the scene calmly. As she stood before him, he greeted her with an understanding expression. No heated exchange. No explanation demanded. Just mercy, empathy and forgiveness. He sent her to dry her eyes. It was a precious gift of compassion worth revealing all those years later.

The first funeral I ever attended was at the age of fifteen. The impression it left was permanent because the deceased was also fifteen. Her name was Missy. She was not my close friend, but a fellow class member who adored music class and singing. We stood next to each other and were elated the day we learned our talent had placed us both in a special singing ensemble. Late that afternoon, her mother's car was hit from behind, slamming it into a light pole, killing Missy. The shock that someone my own age could die left me dazed. Like many music students, I felt drawn to her funeral service. But once there, I sat apart while my eyes swept in the unfamiliar scene before me: the family, the mourners and a minister. I failed to sing along with an unfamiliar hymn. When the minister spoke, it became clear to me he knew Missy personally. She had been a member of his church. He talked about her and the kind of

The Full Ripened Grain

helpful girl she was. In light of her faith, he said, we could rejoice. REJOICE? None of it made sense to me. Missy was dead.

In my hand I held a leaflet. Inside was printed Missy's birth and death dates, the names of the organist and soloist, and the Twenty-third Psalm. I did not know scriptures well, but I knew it was from the Bible. "I will dwell in the house of the Lord forever," it read. FOREVER?

When I got home, I sat alone in my bedroom, thinking. Picking up a pen, I opened the funeral leaflet and wrote on the blank interior:

"Think Benay. Do you realize that if you were killed suddenly like Missy, there would be no one but a stranger to say something for you? You haven't a church or pastor to remember you and tell of any devotion to your church, God or fellow man."

I felt ashamed but was unable to understand why.

I wrote on: "You were extremely embarrassed when you were called upon to sing for the memory of a friend because you didn't even know the words. You faked it. Are you going to fake belief in God, too? Find yourself, Benay. Learn what you want in the worship of a superior being you are not sure exists. Be sure. You say to yourself that religion embarrasses you. People cannot all be alone to pay respect to their god. They do find a kind of solace in it. You try too, Benay. You try too."

*Honor your father and your mother
that your days may be long upon the land
which the Lord your God is giving you.*

– Exodus 20:12

HOME IS WHERE THE HURT IS

An ancient photograph of my father startles me, the image so far from modern times, though we are separated by just a single generation. He is a three-year-old sitting atop a mule in 1923. He wears a straw hat against the hot rural Mississippi sun. My young grandfather stands with his arms around his son. But he squints in the sunlight, making him look irritated and solemn in what must have been a cheerful moment—family photos in the back pasture.

Standing nearby is my great-grandfather, his infant granddaughter—my Aunt Blanche—perched on his arm. His hat obscures his face, the shadow completely blocking the look of his eyes. All I can see is his mustache and pointed chin, a rather mysterious-looking character in a dark

The Full Ripened Grain

jacket and pants. It would be nice to see his eyes. We never met.

I did, however, meet my grandfather on several occasions but I can count on one hand the number of times I can remember seeing him. I grew up a nation away from him in California. We were too middle class and my parents too busy working to afford the time and expensive cross-country trips very often. That is what happens when sons leave their fathers. Their children miss the past. We miss knowing why we are the way we are.

I am touched by the image of these men and their babies. Not a mama in sight. I imagine my grandmother was on the other side of the camera. I also imagine her pride in these people she loved. Sadly, the pride my grandfather had is not evident in his expression nor in the little bit I know about his relationship with my father.

Only sepia-colored photos remain to tell me something of my father's childhood. The toddler grew into a five-year-old who started piano lessons, while his devoted mother sold eggs to pay for lessons. He reached eleven and his folks gave him a shotgun for his birthday. He had a suit with short pants. He became a charming, talented teenager, a mother's pride. His slim class annual attests he was voted "most popular boy" in his class. He was the bonfire around whom the other kids gathered to sing and dance swing and boogie woogie. His impact was such that some of the same people would gather around him at his funeral sixty years later.

He believed in God and sang His praises. He grew up in the Baptist church where gospel quartets traveling the southern states for performance competitions sought his accompaniment and his warm personality,

Coming of age in the Great Depression was tough. Clashing with his father made it tougher. Jobs and cash were scarce. Information was even scarcer. The Sears catalog might be the only place a boy could see what men and women looked like in their underwear. Inexplicably, he could not win his father's respect no matter what he did. In a long-ago moment in a Mississippi forest, they gathered wood, the father irritated by his son, as usual.

"Pick up the pace, boy, can't you move any faster? You can carry more than that."

"Can't you move any faster?" my father said, parroting him.

My grandfather erupted, beating his boy and yelling, "Don't you ever mock me!"

The boy who had been held gently on the mule by his father told him then, "Don't ever touch me again."

In the later years of the Depression, my father worked in CCC camps, the brainstorm of FDR's New Deal to get young men working. He built parks and campsites and kept books for the

The Full Ripened Grain

projects. He was a gifted typist, his piano dexterity called into action on another front.

When World War II called, he went away from home for the first time. My grandmother recorded it in her Bible, her careful penmanship listing the most significant moments in the family's lives: births, deaths, and departures—which are a kind of death.

"Irvin Blakely Hudson left home the 12th day of August 1942 and enlisted for the Navy and was sworn in at Jackson, Mississippi August 13, 1942. Arrived in San Diego, Cal, August 17th." She does not record that he came home shortly afterwards. The explanation is that he is 4-F because of a heart murmur. He got a job and some time passed before he looked up a vivacious, attractive brunette he had met five years earlier when she was a mere twelve years of age. She was Wanda Florene Willingham, living across the state line in Demopolis, Alabama with her parents and three brothers. It was a brief courtship. He was twenty-three and she was seventeen when they married in June, 1944.

Six months later, my mother's mother, my little Alabama granny, at four feet eleven inches, stood in front of her daughter's six-foot, two-inch father-in-law and demanded that he speak to his son. It seemed that after six months, the marriage had not been consummated, with the results being an unsettling shame and embarrassment for both sets of parents. No one talked about such matters openly. There were no magazines in grocery stores

Home is Where The Hurt is

telling customers at the checkout stand how husbands and wives could please each other in bed. The innocence of the media on radio, then television, and the definitions of obscenity in publishing left a mighty silence on the subject of sex. I can only imagine my grandfather's humiliation. I know nothing of the confrontation that followed except for the results.

My sister, Brenda, was born in January, 1946, leading the Baby Boom generation. It was an era of hope following World War II for the nation and our family. It was darkened only by the death of my father's adoring mother, six months after Brenda was born. With her death, my father lost his greatest supporter.

Mom and Dad did their part in the post-war Baby Boom. Beverly was born in 1948. I arrived in 1950.

We three little girls soaked up love from our parents and extended family in Meridian, where we lived, and fifty miles away in Alabama where our maternal grandparents lived. Our healthy young mother naturally abstained from alcohol and tobacco. She nursed us with her full breasts till we could hold a cup and infused us with good health and attachment through years of tender care and garden-grown nourishment.

She cooked from scratch as she had been taught. It was years before any boxed convenience food found its way into our home. The table was perpetually covered in fresh spinach, mustard

The Full Ripened Grain

greens, collard greens, squash, fried chicken, and biscuits that never came from a can. We ate fresh tomatoes, black-eyed peas, green beans, rice and corn. And the cornbread! Not sweet, it was baked in a hot cast iron frying pan and cut into wedges. We ate it hot with butter and sometimes syrup. We crumbled the leftovers into a glass of milk and ate it as cold cereal. Mom's fanciest dessert was banana pudding with meringue. Sometimes it was just simple—but luscious—peaches and cream.

We had a car and a modest new house. My father was a bus driver in segregated Mississippi. The job held no revelations about race or equality for my father. He accepted the status quo as normal, like most of his peers. It was a good, steady job. But he was not satisfied. He heard reports from his sister about sunny California and the abundant, better paying jobs. And there was the lure of a big city where there could be some privacy and anonymity, away from home where everybody knew everybody's business.

My mother agreed to leave Mississippi, believing it was her duty to follow her husband. She tried hard to make him happy, serving hot dinners at noon when Dad came home for lunch. Our pinafores were starched and ironed. Our floors were spotless. Her curious neighbor, Sally, watched her toil.

"You make me tired," Sally would say, and return home to open a can of soup for her husband.

Home is Where The Hurt is

To my mother's consternation, Sally was rewarded with lavish affection from her adoring husband. Dad offered her no such reward. Maybe the move to California was the answer. It was 1952.

We made our way to sprawling Los Angeles in a new Buick with little cash. Streetcars still existed on rails at the time and my father learned to drive one. At their demise, he drove buses again. We moved again and again in a succession of modest but tidy rental homes and duplexes. My sisters and I attended different schools each year throughout our elementary years. It saddened us to move so often, but my father's restlessness could not be satisfied or understood. As young as I was, I knew when there was a crisis at home.

Memories absorbed by a five-year-old can wait long years for understanding. Daddy did not come home one night. The next morning, there was trouble in our house I could sense but no one talked to me about it. My mother looked puzzled and upset, but calm. Outside our house, a car drove up. It was my aunt's car. Daddy emerged from the car, rounded the fender quickly and, keeping his head down, eyes on the ground, he hurried past my mother without a word, almost running into our house. No one stopped me, so I hurried after Daddy into the house, into my parents' room where I saw him fling himself across the double bed, burying his face in the pillows. He sobbed, his face red and contorted. I stood close by the bed quietly, concerned and sorry for him. Instinctively, I reached out and patted him on his shoulder. He caught me up in his arms and hugged me tightly, still crying. I didn't know why he had been gone, only that he was back and that he was sorry and so sad.

Brenda told me, years later, "That was the night Dad was arrested."

Arrested? I didn't ask why.

******

The sides of my father's personality were like beveled glass and just as fragile. We tiptoed around him, fearing his quick temper and his criticism. He seemed so damned angry most of the time. Alternately, he had a charming facet of good-natured humor that caught the light and was available to the public and friends. And us, too.

His love for us was clear, when he was affectionate and in a good mood. But we feared his wrath. He was picky and demanding and self-conscious about his style, his wife's style and ours. Until the day he died, whenever we met, I felt that I was being critiqued on my personal appearance. He noticed my too-short skirts when I was young and pointed out my gray hairs when I was older. He always seemed to feel he had that right.

Our California childhood gave us access to people and places our parents couldn't imagine while still in Mississippi. Dad's sister, Blanche,

Home is Where The Hurt is

married a wealthy older man in 1955 and the associated friends brought glamour to our lives. We were not far from Hollywood and some of my aunt's friends were in the entertainment industry. Aunt Blanche's friends provided us with tickets to television show tapings. We went to the NBC and CBS studios and watched show business legends perform for live audiences. Fred Astaire, Dinah Shore, Bob Hope. All for free! Dad and Mom were invited to the Moulin Rouge, a famous night club, and even took us girls there to a special performance by Sammy Davis Jr. A photographer took our picture seated at the table in our frilly dresses.

Dad escorted my mother to a job interview as hostess for The Old Virginia Steak House in Pasadena in 1957. He waited for her in the cocktail lounge where an empty piano bench and keyboard beckoned.

"Do you play?" a patron asked.

"Yes," he said.

With no sheet music, Dad played by ear each requested song. They raved.

The manager offered Dad a job on the spot, $200 a week. He could work half the time of his day job for twice the money. He left the secure but mundane life of a bus system supervisor. Playing the piano at night in restaurant lounges and piano bars became his full-time profession. He became a member of the musicians union, a pro with a twenty-five year career ahead of him. Eventually,

The Full Ripened Grain

my mother became a hostess in a restaurant on La Cienega Boulevard, which was called Restaurant Row by Los Angelenos. Mom was attractive and some customers said she reminded them of movie star Jane Russell. It flattered her and she gained poise and confidence to add to her natural Southern charm and modest good manners. She greeted and seated stars and bragged she had more than one escorted out the door of the elegant place for drunkenness. Our income increased.

Aunt Blanche was pleased. She was my father's best friend. He admired her fine brunette beauty, how well she wore expensive clothes, her wit, humor and charm. Some of these were traits he admired in my mother as well, at least at first. But she failed to live up to the cool standards achieved by Blanche, her privileged life and her popular friends. Dad retained an intimacy with his sister that left my mother out. Despite her new employment, Mom was naïve and a little square, still the country girl from Mississippi trying to find her place in a sophisticated society.

Sunday became their only day off work. Church attendance faltered. But family time and Sunday remained strong. A new car and Sunday meant Sunday drives, a mandatory event. Dad knew every corner in Los Angeles and Hollywood, knowledge left over from his trolley and bus driving days. We kids fought for a window seat and watched all of LA and its suburbs roll by. We were treated to ice cream or the new food fad,

Home is Where The Hurt is

pizza pie. We put our feet in the stars' handprints at Grauman's Chinese Theater. We visited Forest Lawn Cemetery and saw the graves of famous people. Our parents directed our eyes to copies of great European works of art that dotted the landscape there. Sometimes we went with Dad by ourselves and sat on Hollywood Boulevard and just watched people. We were pals.

On one such outing, we walked by a jewelry store window in Hollywood. Beverly and I, heads together, looked at an unusual piece on display.

"Isn't that a queer ring?" I said to Beverly.

"Don't EVER use that word," Dad barked at me, angrily. I did not understand why, but I remembered it always.

Because they were both working at night, Mom and Dad left Brenda in charge of us and bedtime as early as the age of eleven. Although Brenda was only two years older than Beverly, we usually respected her authority. It cast her in a role of responsibility and control, a burden from which she has never been free. She mothered us, taking on what was surely serious responsibility for a child her age. Brenda got us ready for bed and curled our hair for school the next day. And we obeyed, leaving the black and white television after Zorro or the night's favorite show was over.

We kept in touch with our extended family as much as we could. Expensive long distance phone calls were rare. We exchanged letters, waiting for signs they remembered us and we were never disappointed. Christmas packages and then Christmas cards with money arrived. There were boxes of shelled pecans hand-picked by our granddaddy. I imagined him sitting on the porch of his modest brick home surrounded by heaps of pecan hulls.

Our biggest thrill was the Christmas delivery of a coconut cake baked by our granny. She called it a Japanese fruit cake. Four layers high, it alternated layers of raisin spice cake and yellow cake filled with pecans. The sugary coconut icing was decorated with pecan halves and candied cherries in red and green. It was a magnificent miracle that made it through the mail a little shaken but intact. The effort to bake and wrap that cake seemed monumental and a sign our faraway grandmother loved us and remembered us. We were connected as a family. Many years later, she would tell me, "I never forgave them for taking y'all away from us."

Dad attempted to bridge the uncomfortable gap between him and his father. My grandfather took the train to Los Angeles twice and seemed mellow and pleased with his children's lives as they evolved in Southern California. All seemed well.

Then Dad was hired in 1959 to play piano in an LA suburb called West Covina. We moved again. My parents bought a three-bedroom tract home that needed work. Mom took a job during the day at a retail clothing store. She had the personality and fashion sense to make a success of it and eventually became store manager. She was a young

Home is Where The Hurt is

woman in her thirties and finally started to recognize her own talents.

As she matured, more tension developed between her and Dad. He ridiculed her. Her hair wasn't right, her bra was too "pointy" and she was too thin. Even while she was earning more, the new house and the needs of three growing children caused money problems. They began to argue about everything. Dad would bellow, "We made $16,000 this year and what have we got to show for it?"

Their roles had been reversed. Mom was the daytime breadwinner and went off to work each day after we left for school. She managed the dress shop and became active in the chamber of commerce, attending events and helping with promotions for the Plaza Shopping Center.

At home during the day, Dad took over. He was an excellent gardener. Our house included a wide backyard overwhelmed by weeds and knee-high grass. Dad tore at the weeds and reseeded our backyard, his green thumb in high gear. Bright pink geraniums lined the parking strip in front of our house. Carpet-like cool dichondra covered the lawn. Red bottlebrush, pink bougainvillea, orange birds of paradise, yellow roses, and sweet white lemon blossoms opened in our yard.

Dad's flair for cooking made him a kitchen nag, hovering over my mother's shoulder suggesting this or that. It infuriated her. It was hard to work all day on her feet and get a meal on the table before

The Full Ripened Grain

Dad had to get ready for his evening job. One evening Mom made shortcake with strawberries. Cooking hastily, she forgot to add the baking powder to the shortcake. She served it anyway. Using his fork, Dad tapped the tough cake with his fork, not in good-natured teasing, but in cruel mockery. Despite a day of managing a store, she had come home to failure. But there were traditional roles to be upheld and she tried. She kept house with the help of us girls, training us early how to start a meal and clean up. We washed laundry, ironed, cleaned our rooms, and took turns doing the dishes. Mom returned home at 5:30 most nights to complete a meal we had started. And then Dad took over the kitchen. His timing was rigid, hardly giving Mom a moment after coming in the door to catch her breath and wash her hands before calling us to the table. It didn't help anyone's digestion.

When Dad reached the age of forty, the problems between him and my mother escalated. The cause was still mysterious to me at age eleven. I never saw any cuddling or affection between them. When I visited my girlfriend's house, I marveled at how her father would lean over their living room chair and schmooch his wife's cheek, sputtering and kissing and making her laugh right in front of us! My girlfriend was embarrassed but I was fascinated and charmed by it. That never happened at home. There were moments of camaraderie between my parents but I never saw a

Home is Where The Hurt is

romantic moment. When each departed for a trip, there would be a chaste kiss on the lips, but never anything more. I never saw my father embrace my mother in a full-bodied hug or steal a kiss at the kitchen sink.

Dad began to make new friends at work and brought them home to meet us. They were often single men. Always gracious and welcoming, Mom enjoyed their occasional visits too. My parents impressed me by maintaining a tradition of Southern hospitality and good humor in the face of any strain or financial pressure. People liked them a lot.

My girlfriends liked them too and liked being at our house for overnight slumber parties on weekends. Among the three of us, there might be a dozen girls or more stretched out in blankets and sleeping bags on the living room floor. Mom tolerated the noise. One friend told me how sweet my mother was when she "yelled" at us to quiet down and go to sleep. Working nights, Dad avoided the female fracas. He came home from his piano bar at 2:30 a.m., stepping carefully through the sleeping bags on the carpet, the house littered with slumber party carnage.

But the worst thing we could have done to our father began to happen. We turned into young women.

The onslaught of raging female hormones had him surrounded. He bristled at the eye makeup, bouffant hairdos, and early sixties fashions that made Brenda look older and sexier than her years should have allowed. I listened as he insulted her. Dad suspected the worst intentions of any male who came to visit. His gruff demeanor embarrassed us in front of our friends.

It is a Saturday night in 1963. Dad has gone to the piano bar to play for the night. No sooner does he leave than Brenda does too, against his strict orders. She is a rebel at 16, looking for independence. I am stricken with anxiety.

There is the sound of Dad's car returning and suddenly, a pounding on the patio glass door—a frightening urgency to it, as if the glass will break. Since I have locked the front door, our father cannot immediately get into the house. I am struck stupid, not knowing which angry pounding to answer, the front door or the patio.

I soon learn that in a scene similar to *Ferris Bueller's Day Off*, Brenda has sprinted home, hoping to beat Dad's car to the driveway. Only it is not funny. She is just moments too slow. Caught.

I retreat to my bedroom—berated by my sister for my disloyalty and dull-wittedness. All I can hear is Dad's roar. I am a failure to both of them: a bad daughter for not telling my father about Brenda's disobedience, and a lousy accomplice.

Mom sympathized and trusted us. She wanted us to enjoy our high school years.

At school, we flourished. Away from home, we each enjoyed our own roles and success. All three of us grasped on to our girlfriends and school life

Home is Where The Hurt is

as a life preserver in the sea of tension that began to exist in our home.

Five years ahead of me, Brenda seemed so grown up, singing solos in a black sheath and pearls. Academically, she soared. Beverly sang and acted as well, the two of them popular for their personalities and talent. The good grades we all achieved were taken for granted. Our parents had other things on their minds. Besides, no one in our family had ever gone to college, so there was no pressure about qualifying.

There is a black and white Kodak Brownie snapshot of my mom and dad taken at this time. They are dressed up and standing near our front porch. Dad wears a suit and squints into the sunlight, a brooding expression on his face. He stands adrift, separated from my mother who is posing with her head held high in the erect posture she always struck while being photographed. She is lovely in her Kennedy-era V-necked sheath with three-quarter sleeves. Her brunette hair is collar-length and curled. Dad must have been the only guy in town who didn't find her attractive.

Our one-story ranch-style house was long and narrow. You could see the hallways from almost any room in the house, and sounds easily carried. During a sad day in the decline of my parents' marriage, I was on the opposite side of the house from them, taking a shower. Turning off the water, I opened the shower door and reached for a towel. It was startling to hear the rough muffled voices of

The Full Ripened Grain

my parents. I hurried to dress and approached the hallway slowly, not able to understand anything being said except the tone. It was angry. The sound drew me in and I knew I was trespassing. Instead of running away, I walked boldly toward their bedroom door. Then I heard it—a slap. I opened the door and saw my mother collapse onto their bed, sobbing.

"Call the police. Call the police!" Mom cried out.

I didn't move. I didn't make the call. There was no 911 in those days. Maybe I didn't know how to do it. My father was standing there, but I can't recall what he said or did. I can only remember that I did not think my mother really meant what she said. Call the police? On my father, whom I loved? I was an obedient girl and always did what my mother told me to do. But I ignored this request. The whole scene just didn't make any sense. I loved both of them. And I knew beyond a doubt both of them loved me. Why couldn't they love each other?

"You were the only one who cried," Beverly told me later.

It was her frank assessment of the end of our parents' marriage that had come as no surprise to her. But what she said was not true. I saw my mother cry, arms thrown dramatically around the neck of my old Uncle Charlie who offered solace. Her shoulders shook as she sobbed. My father did not want her. He wanted something else.

Home is Where The Hurt is

She helped move Dad's things into his own apartment, not very far away from our house. Shutting the door on him and their marriage had broken her heart. And it broke mine.

*I look behind me and you're there,
then up ahead and you're there, too—
Your reassuring presence, coming and going.*

– Psalm 139:5-6

GRADUATION USA

I must have been the only girl at high school graduation who had a cheering squad comprised of my mother, sisters, father and father's lover. My future husband was also seated with them. The years past and the years to come were all laid out in front of me in the form of these people who loved me and hoped for me.

Still seventeen, I was filled with knowledge of English, civics and world history, but not the awareness of contemporary social upheaval. Despite all I had witnessed, I was surprisingly innocent. I accepted this incarnation of my personal circle with affection. I could see their smiling faces in the crowd, so happy and proud while I sang a duet, "Sunrise, Sunset," with my friend, Danny:

*Is this the little girl I carried?
Is this the little boy at play?*

Graduation USA

I don't remember growing older,
When did they?
...Sunrise, sunset, sunrise, sunset, swiftly
fly the years–
One season following another, laden with
happiness and tears.

How prophetic it was. It was 1968 and the year was one of the most extraordinary in the life of the country. Dr. Martin Luther King was assassinated in April. The nation had hardly grasped the impact of this event when Senator Robert Kennedy was shot on the night of his triumph in the California presidential primary. It felt so personal for us, who could easily recall our feelings at the death of President Kennedy. Dad woke me with a phone call at 2 a.m. to tell me. He had just finished a piano set at work when the news broke. The volatile Democratic convention heated up that summer. Boys in my class left to fight the Vietnam War. Richard Nixon won the White House and with it, a generational civil war of sorts. Even a self-centered teen like me knew the nation was hurting.

The Feminine Mystique, by Betty Freidan, was five years old and its sentiment of restless womanhood was finding its way into my generation. What kind of career might I have? My mother had worked at a salaried job since I was little. I assumed I would have to earn a living too. Both my mother and Brenda were divorced by

The Full Ripened Grain

then. Marriage held little sense of security for me. I could not and would not assume I would marry and that a man would always be there, taking care of me.

My father did not take care of me financially. At the time of their divorce, a loan my parents owed needed to be repaid. In exchange for child support, my father agreed to pay it. Foolishly, my mother gave up our house, to split the profit with my father. Beverly and I remained in our mother's custody as teenagers. All of us, including Brenda and daughter Dawn, from her brief marriage, stuffed ourselves into a two-bedroom apartment. I simply rolled with whatever wave washed over us.

I had bright friends and we played at being very grown up, renting an apartment in Balboa Beach for a week following graduation. Where would our lives lead? I did not know a single one of us headed straight for college. There was only one among us whose parents had attended college.

Earlier that final school year, a favorite English teacher had hinted at my potential.

"Have you thought about what college you might go to?" asked Mr. Youngerman.

"Not really," I said, feeling baffled and non-committal. The thought had never crossed my mind. Me? Go to college?

With a grade point average of 3.7, I was thirteenth scholastically in a class of 425 students. But my counselor at school and my parents never

Graduation USA

mentioned further education for me. It was simply not in the family culture.

On that graduation day, Dad said, "Now you can get yourself a good little job as a secretary."

I fumed inwardly, angry at his traditional expectations for me. Was that all he could dream for me? However essential a good secretary is, these were the jobs to which all women had been assigned for ages. I had a hunger to learn more and he just didn't get it.

I was not alone in this. My good friend, Maria, said her father believed college was useless, that she would just get married and have children. He would not pay for it. She took advantage of the tuition-free California community colleges and took classes where instructors encouraged her to complete a B.A. She went on to law school and became an attorney in Washington, D.C. where she lobbied on labor issues. Her father was right about one thing. She got married and had a child. And fifteen years later, a divorce.

My friend, Leslie, was a whiz at math. She wanted four years of it in high school in order to qualify for selective colleges. But our mutual high school counselor said no. She had to complete Senior Home Economics. It was required. Calculus would not fit into the schedule. So she took the math in summer school and went off to college, eventually earning a Ph.D. in psychology. She has a private practice in Oregon.

The Full Ripened Grain

We talked about this in later years, the school counselors with blinders who saw middle-class kids with no particular vision in mind. We needed someone to tell us we were smart.

In the school library, I found a brochure for a state college, but even the $1200 annual fees sounded like a lot of money. When I showed the brochure to Dad, he said he didn't think we could afford that. I showed it to my optimistic mom and she said, "Let's get one of those student loans."

Mercy, peace and love be yours in abundance.

– Jude 1:2

DATELINE: ENUMCLAW

Growing up in suburban Southern California, the closest I came to agriculture was the strawberry fields that still skirted our neighborhood. I hadn't a clue how they were cultivated, but they showed up regularly for sale in little stands by the road. Our family bought bulging pints of the red berries wrapped in brown paper. Orange groves that had been abundant in Covina and West Covina were being leveled for new homes within easy commuting distance of Los Angeles. Disneyland took up a big hunk of Orange County when it was built, but we were happy to be there the day after it opened in 1955. Mom and Dad were good to us that way.

Then there was my dad's fight with a banana tree uprooting our front porch on California Street. It was exotic to say the least, and Dad's upbringing with rural Mississippi crops and gardens was no match for this jungle plant. I ate the strawberries and watched Daddy hack at the banana tree. His cussing-sprinkled labor failed to impress my sisters and me with the joy of gardening. We were given the chore of picking cut worms out of the dichondra. He never showed me how to plant a flower.

I had no particular sense about the importance of agriculture or livestock. Even though I lived in "The Breadbasket of the World," and one of the nation's leading dairy states, I could not tell the difference between, say, a Holstein cow and a Jersey. I was a real heifer.

This became all too apparent when, as newlyweds, my husband Lynn and I made the decision to move northward to a small dairy-farming community in Washington State.

The move was for the sake of Lynn's young career in city management. It was a traumatic departure for our families, who considered this move a temporary folly. For me it was simple. We had no children yet, few belongings, and a desire to live in a climate with real seasons. It also put twelve hundred miles between me and my splintered family. They would find their own path. I never realized how rocky it would be. For the time being, the excitement of a new marriage and a new job made it easy for me to leave them behind.

******

Dateline: Enumclaw

When I arrived at the *Enumclaw Courier-Herald* in 1973, I was fresh from college with my new degree in communications. Having spent a year working in Los Angeles, the change to rural Washington took some cultural adjustment, a euphemism for keeping your mouth shut.

"Just give it some time," Robert Olson, the benevolent editor of the city's weekly newspaper, told me. "Just watch and learn and don't try too hard."

My husband, with his equally fresh degree, had been hired as the new assistant city administrator. We checked into King's Motel and were greeted warmly by the clerk, who said she had read about us in the newspaper. We were stunned that our arrival warranted publicity—anywhere.

As a writer, I had hoped for a career in the media—copywriting for an ad agency or television news production. There were no such opportunities in Enumclaw. The long highway to Seattle seemed, at the time, a little treacherous. And so I came to the *Courier-Herald* and was immediately made a part-time reporter by Mr. Olson.

Robert Olson was a towering Swede. He edited the *Enumclaw Courier-Herald* for thirty years, guarding its integrity from his glassed-in office on Cole Street. Mr. Olson was tall and imposing like the Douglas firs that surround the little northwest city. Ironically, his friends called him "Bud." Hovering over the staff at six feet, four inches, he surely weighed three hundred pounds. His big bay-

The Full Ripened Grain

window chest filled his editor's chair from side to side. Nearly seventy, he was still a sturdy man in his Florsheim wingtips and dress trousers. He usually chose a cardigan sweater to wear over a collared shirt and tie. His long pale cheeks had creased and his dark hair had grayed. His bushy eyebrows and kindly eyes gazed at me over the glasses perched on his nose, giving him a grandfatherly demeanor. I never could have called him "Bud."

Mr. Olson was worldly but loved his small-town home. He was born there in 1911. Except for his education at Stanford and a tour of duty in the peacetime navy, his focus and loyalties seemed to rest on Washington State and in particular, Enumclaw.

His weekly column was informal and he mused on anything he could spot from his office or by peering left to right out the two storefront windows at the building's entrance. It was disconcerting for some of his readers to see their personal errands and private business made the subject of a newspaper column. Their movements were forever recorded in the bound editions of the *Courier-Herald* kept in the basement of the Enumclaw Library. He was not fazed by his subjects' indignant complaints.

His column was also a forum for writing about his domestic hobbies of cooking and gardening. In a city where the majority of men were tough loggers, dairy farmers, pickle packers, and insurance executives, his recipe for Irish soda bread may have been less-than-intriguing subject matter. But there were enough genteel souls in Enumclaw to appreciate the homages to asparagus and bread batter and diatribes about using real butter rather than margarine.

His commentary on the weather was printed and spoken in the *C-H* office. Summer days of "relentless sunshine" were tough on him and made him as uncomfortable and ornery as the polar bears at Point Defiance Zoo in Tacoma. On a drizzling July morning, Mr. Olson would walk majestically through the front door of the office and bellow, "Isn't it a beautiful morning?"

He did not confide in me about his loneliness, but I knew his wife was in a nursing home, suffering from a degenerative disease. He visited her regularly and returned to the office without much comment. His two grown children lived and worked far away and we heard little about them. There were rumors of a rift between him and his son, Bruce, who had become infamous during Vietnam anti-war protests at the University of Washington. As editor of the counter-culture infused UW *Daily*, the young Olson had challenged and shaken the foundation of his father's conservative framework. He used the student newspaper as a weapon against the Nixon administration's foreign policies. Watergate had not yet dampened support for the president.

The Full Ripened Grain

Freedom of the press survived in its own fashion in Enumclaw, resting on the shoulders of the gentlemanly Mr. Olson. Change in social matters was hard for him.

******

One of the most profitable December promotions at the paper was the business sponsorship honoring the first baby of the New Year. A shower of gifts and publicity for the new parents and baby awaited. Businesses catering to families bought advertising space in the special edition.

Up until the year I covered the story, no one had anticipated that the first baby of the year at Community Memorial Hospital might possibly be born to a single parent. In 1970s Enumclaw, she was still referred to as an "unwed mother."

The Love Generation was reaching parenting age if not voluntary marrying age. The fallout was reaching Enumclaw and a newspaper editor who was not sympathetic. However, a Love Generation representative was reporting for the *Courier-Herald*. I was on the beat.

Midnight had passed. The New Year had arrived and a newborn lay in its bassinet in the hospital nursery with only its mother's name on the I.D. card. A giveaway.

"What are the odds?" I sighed, knowing instinctively this was a potential public relations

Dateline: Enumclaw

problem for the ad manager and the editor. But the prizes were to go to the first baby, not the first baby with two parents who were legally married.

As soon as it was polite, I approached the young mom and asked the pertinent questions. I determined that the baby's father was "unavailable for comment." The newborn had its precious aura, which was enough for me. I took their picture.

On fire with righteousness, I returned to the office ready to defend the Truth against small town censorship. I reasoned that every individual born deserves to be celebrated despite his parents' circumstances. And who needs more help with supplies than a single parent? Should the matter come up, that is. I felt righteous but not brave. Mr. Olson scared me a little.

Mr. Olson took my write-up. I said nothing. He edited it and the cutline under the picture of the young woman and her baby, which I had purposely left ambiguous. Nothing was printed to suggest there might not be a "Mr. Smith," who just might have declined to have his photo taken. Freedom of the Press, for me at least, also meant not reporting the whole truth. It was the best I could do for the ad manager and his clients. As for Mr. Olson, his only comment was a perturbed, "See if you can get me a married mother next time."

My assignment took me over the county line to a rival city, Buckley. I thought of myself as the "foreign correspondent." Buckley, population 4,000, is located four miles away from Enumclaw and just

The Full Ripened Grain

across the White River, which marks the county line. It could be said I was in the right place at the right time—depending on one's view of Buckley.

Only a short time earlier, the century-old *Buckley News Banner* had been sold to the publisher of the *Courier-Herald*. It was a source of bitter resentment toward the newspaper by the good people of Buckley. Old rivalries persisted, especially in high school sports. There I sat in the empty store front of the old newspaper building, taking classified ads and local news handwritten on college rule notebook paper. Daily, I brought a thermos of coffee and a spiral bound reporters' notebook and a camera ready for Buckley newsgathering. I had a desk with a telephone and a cavernous empty print shop behind me.

There was no news wire service at the newspaper since we did not handle much state and national news. But in 1973, there was also no fax machine, no cell phone, no desktop computer, and no internet.

It was my job to cover local events and the White River School District. As the wife of a local city administrator, any coverage of Enumclaw or Buckley city politics would have been, well, tainted. Public relations became my strong suit. I began any interview by acknowledging the loss the community had suffered at the hands of the newspaper I represented. They knew I was a stranger to the area and as such, had no history with either town. It was up to me to cultivate their trust. But the good

Dateline: Enumclaw

citizens of Buckley had a chip on their shoulders the size of the logs they cut down.

It was a bit lonely, but so much a change from the life I had known that it all fascinated me. I settled into the routine life of not-so-routine reporting. I put our 35mm Pentax to use on the job. The first day I forgot it, a llama came walking down the middle of Main Street. The animals were a new fad among many large property owners, but one seldom saw them beyond their corrals. Lesson learned.

I had a talent for composition, if not lighting. Having taken photography at college, I had knowledge of dark room procedures and had learned to live with the rotten-egg-smelling chemicals used to process black and white film. There were no union restrictions at a weekly. I wrote, photographed, developed, and printed photos to publish with the accounts of local drama and puff pieces. All the reporters did. Both of us.

I learned quickly that photographic achievement has as much to do with the will to shoot as it does with equipment and ability. I covered the Buckley Logger's Rodeo. There would be competition among area loggers, including a pole climb. Loggers were the cowboys of the towns and woe to the ignorant person who snickered at the burly guys striding across the street in flannel plaid shirts and Levis cut off and ragged at mid-calf. Their ankle-high steel-toed work boots reminded me of Li'l Abner in the

The Full Ripened Grain

comics. But I soon learned that the short pants meant a safer operation for the men who set choker chains around enormous felled trees. It was no laughing matter and very dangerous work.

I anticipated the big event with fantasies of a photo page with my byline. The pole climb contest was getting underway with two parallel tree trunks having been erected. The first logger to scale his tree, ring the bell at the top, and get back to the ground would be the winner. I steadied my camera. Two competitors approached the poles. Each wore large belt-like harnesses at his hips. The harness encircled the trunk of the tree. They wore corked boots with knife-like spikes protruding from their insteps. A signal sounded and they leaped, their boots slamming into the sides of the trunk. Lifting the harness high around the poles, the men dug their boot spikes into the bark and yanked, hoisting themselves up, up, up, thirty feet in the air until DING! The bell sounded. My camera was focused at the top of the tree trunk. I watched, terrified, as one man's boots lost its grip. He plunged downward, the belted harness catching the pole fitfully, slowing, but not stopping his fall.

I screamed. I closed my eyes, put my hands over my face and turned away. My camera and responsibility were cast aside. The logger thudded to the ground, flat on his back, onto soft sawdust. He survived. I nearly didn't.

******

Dateline: Enumclaw

The prestigious Dairy Family of the Year was announced annually by the Washington Dairy Products Commission. At that time dairy farms dotted the entire Enumclaw plateau. It was no surprise when the Anderson family was chosen for the honor. A photo session was in order. I arranged the date and arrived at the farmhouse with high hopes for a simple portrait. Warm and friendly, the family obliged politely as I arranged Mr. and Mrs. Anderson and their teenagers in various poses. I was touched at how my two-year stint at the newspaper made me a well-known figure to most homes. They trusted me. Their regard and cooperation was complete. I sensed a mutual respect and affection from this dear and accomplished family. It was a satisfying session all around.

Back in the darkroom, I pressed the release button on the bottom of the camera and began turning the crank to rewind the film. There was no resistance. I turned and turned the little crank, praying for the telltale click of the final release of the film. There was none. There was no film in the camera.

My Pentax had become an appendage of my shoulder in the daily work of reporting. Putting film in and taking film out was as much a part of my daily duties as brushing my teeth. It was a steadfast personal rule that once film was rewound and expelled from the camera, another roll went in. I was never without it. Except this time.

The Full Ripened Grain

How it happened was irrelevant. The fact was I had to take those photos again. I felt humiliated. I was so downhearted that I called my new best girlfriend to tell her what had happened. Her name was Judy and she was a peach. Her sense of humor and her compassion were what I needed and she provided them. The situation was actually quite funny and she made me laugh about it. But I was loath to admit it, certainly not to Mr. Olson.

A day or so later, I summoned my courage to call the Andersons and tell them I would have to come again. The photos had "not turned out," which was quite true.

I underestimated the small town grapevine that couldn't keep a story like that buried. Without me knowing it, Judy talked with her father on the phone and told him my sorrowful tale. He then visited his neighbor Mr. Anderson and spilled the beans.

Seemingly safe with my secret, I was effusive with gratitude as I arrived at the Andersons. They graciously welcomed me once again. I muttered something about "technical equipment." I did as much smiling as they did. When the shots had been taken, I thanked them profusely for their patience. Feeling relieved, I headed for the door. There were salutations all around, which ended with Mr. Anderson remarking, "Next time, make sure there is film in your camera."

******

Dateline: Enumclaw

When the regional Junior Livestock Show opened at the Enumclaw fairgrounds, I was sent to cover it. I expected to see a petting zoo of baby animals. I gleefully took my camera and plenty of film to document these little cuties visiting our town.

Instead, I found the fairgrounds bustling with the full-sized variety of farm animals and hundreds of teenagers in Levis and blue shirts with "Future Farmers of America" emblazoned on them. The publicity chairman gave me a thick stapled document listing the three days of events such as "Showing and Fitting" (a fashion show?) and "Judging" (Judge not, lest ye be judged?).

Mr. Porter, a young FFA advisor and teacher from the high school, was kind and willing to help me. He was sympathetic to this city girl and smiled shyly when I admitted I didn't know anything about livestock. Throwing myself at his mercy seemed to be the shortest route to a story. That was when I learned it usually pleases and flatters other people to be regarded as the true experts on themselves and their programs. Because they are. Better to ask an "obvious" question than to assume a wrong answer and put it in print. I felt I could trust him.

Young Mr. Porter in his cowboy hat and denims began a simple but somewhat lengthy explanation of his FFA kids and the 4-H competitions. We stood near a corral that was nearly hidden by six-foot-high solid fencing. He talked and I tried to concentrate, taking notes furiously. But my peripheral vision became distracted by some activity behind the fence. I couldn't help but notice the head of a large black cow rising above the fence like an impromptu puppet show over Mr. Porter's shoulder.

What an enormous cow, I thought. I said nothing. The teacher continued to talk.

The head of the bovine began to bob, its snout pointed upward and eyes half-closed, as if he was standing on two feet dancing, grooving to some cool imagined music. I stared.

Mr. Porter's eyes caught mine and followed them to the scene of the action.

"Oh my," said young Mr. Porter, looking at his booted feet and blushing. The situation finally sank in. I was getting my piece of the story while this bull was getting his. The bull's head sank behind the fence, leaving me with fantasies of bovine afterglow. It wouldn't fit in the story.

The excitement continued in another direction when the grand champion hog appeared for cameras and the press. A few flashes ignited and the hog keeled over. He was as dead as the expression on the bull's face when he sank behind the fence.

******

Apart from my stunning introduction to the world of animal husbandry, Mr. Olson's decision

Dateline: Enumclaw

to hire me led to a cast of characters who became endeared to me. With President Ford in the White House, it was amusing to all who entered the *Courier-Herald* office that Betty Ford took the classified ads and walk-in news at the front desk. Unlike her White House counterpart, Betty did not consider diplomacy vital to her job.

"Hey reporters!" she would yell. "WE GOT SOME GOSSIP UP HERE!"

The well-meaning news source, standing at the counter, usually shrank a little.

Betty's husband was named Henry Ford. Henry kept the presses running, in much the same way that another Henry Ford kept cars rolling off the assembly line. There was not a poster, ticket, menu, invitation, or advertisement that did not run through Henry's machinery. When I arrived at the *Courier-Herald*, it still used a hot-type machine operated by an aging technician named Heime. It was a toss-up as to which was the more antique— the machine or Heime.

Genteel Una Waldron handled the archives and billing. In the open office, she provided a wise counterpoint to the circle of activity around her. Occasionally, a phone call from a reader came with a challenging question. Once, when Betty answered the phone, she put her hand over the speaker and said to Una, "This guy wants to know how to write to the President."

"Tell him to address it to 1600 Pennsylvania Avenue, Washington, D.C.," said Una.

The Full Ripened Grain

"How did you know THAT?" said Betty, incredulous.

Una took another call. "This guy wants to know how old a cow has to be before she freshens," she said to Betty.

"I don't know," said Betty. "I haven't freshened in so long."

******

Life in Enumclaw brought a steady stream of annual events such as the Dairy Princess Pageant. The lovely teenager chosen for the title was not called the Dairy Queen for obvious reasons. It was a big deal since the Enumclaw plateau hosted dozens of dairy farms. I covered the pageants, traveling as far as the Holiday Inn in Everett for the crowning. My reward for the long trip was winning a door prize. I was a little embarrassed to win since I was there as a professional journalist covering the story. The purity of my professional reputation was at stake. But frankly, I needed the twenty pounds of laundry detergent.

Every newspaper has its publicity hounds. At that particular time at the *C-H*, a woman I will call Maxine kept our phones busy. A new reporter was initiated only after fielding several calls from Maxine. Her voice was unmistakable. She had a Brooklyn accent, which was quite uncommon for our region. The accent and its connection to urban city life was the only explanation we had as to why

Dateline: Enumclaw

she called frequently with her urgent, stop-the-presses news and suggestions for a feature story. She seemed overwhelmed by her new rural life.

"Did you know you can eat pumpkins?" she asked earnestly. "Every year there is a shocking and deplorable waste of pumpkins at Halloween."

I suggested she call Mike Wallace at *60 Minutes*.

One spring day, the phone rang again and Maxine's excited voice announced breaking news.

"My chicken eggs have hatched!" she cried. "You should see them! There is one ENORMOUS one."

Well, it must have been a Wednesday, that is to say, the day after deadline and nothing much else was going on. Only that and a desperate need for photos would have prompted me to give in to yet another shaky publicity pitch.

Now I would venture to say there is not a rural weekly reporter who hasn't taken a camera and shot his or her fair share of agricultural oddities such as a gargantuan potato or a mutated tomato suggesting the Madonna. In fact, one early *C-H* reporter photographed a massive sunflower which made it to the syndicated Ripley's Believe it or Not feature. In recent years, journalistic fervor and integrity has snubbed its nose at donated checks being passed from one publicity seeker to another. It isn't very creative and it leaves the reporter feeling a bit

The Full Ripened Grain

used. Still, depending on the circumstances, it does help to illustrate a happy thing.

What could be happier than springtime and baby chicks? So I caved.

I had never met Maxine and had no idea what to expect. She gave me directions to her home, not far out of town. I grabbed my camera and notepad and out the door I went, grateful for anything that made me look industrious.

My little green Mustang stopped in front of a wire fence, outside an old bungalow. The raised porch needed some paint. Standing on the porch was a woman I presumed to be Maxine. I hesitated. She was a little more than middle-aged woman with a head full of salt-and-pepper Shirley Temple ringlets. She wore a black shirtwaist dress with no stockings and tennis shoes. For all of her publicity savvy, news of 1970s fashions had not reached her.

She smiled a greeting and motioned her hand to welcome me through the wire gate. I smiled back and climbed the steep front steps with my camera and strap dangling from my shoulder. I followed her inside. The chickens were inside?

Yes, it was a nice day, we agreed as she led me to the top of the basement stairs. The painted boards creaked as we descended. Light streaming through the basement windows illuminated a corner of the basement where I recognized a poultry cage. Warm lights hung over it. I was relieved. It was a good setup.

Dateline: Enumclaw

"I've been feeding them herbal tea," she told me. I nodded agreeably as if I had heard that before in my life. I gazed upon the cage.

Under the warm lights, a brood of wide-awake, peeping yellow chicks crowded around a feeding cup. Among the yellow fuzz appeared some darker brown fuzz with a more elongated body and tail. It had a sleek head, long neck, a bill, and tiny webbed feet. The enormous chick was a duckling.

My thoughts scrambled for a proper attitude. I was in the basement of a woman whose appearance reminded me of Bette Davis in *What Ever Happened to Baby Jane?* Does she honestly not realize this is a duck? If she doesn't, should I be the one to tell her? Should I chuckle and point out the facts, or would chuckling offend her? For that matter, if I asked, "Are you out of your mind?" would that provoke her?

Hovering in the back of my mind was the realization that no one knew where I was. I had not risked the ridicule of my fellow reporters by admitting, let us say—revealing—my sources. There seemed to be no one upstairs in the house and I was alone in a basement with Bette Davis, uh, Maxine, and she didn't know the difference between a chicken and a duck!

Weighing my options, I took my camera from my shoulder and decided to give Maxine what she expected—a photo shoot. I snapped away, saying nothing about the enormous little "chicken." Portrait photographer Annie Leibovitz would have

The Full Ripened Grain

been proud of me. The wide angles, the lighting, the close-ups. I covered every inch of the cage and its warm glowing lights. Finished and satisfied, I thanked her for her hospitality, but I needed to GET GOING.

The open air had never smelled so good.

A few weeks later, Mr. Olson walked out of his office holding a copy of *The National Inquirer*. I teased him.

"Someone brought this to me—a woman from Enumclaw had a tip published in *The National Inquirer*. 'Oatmeal in your bath is good for the skin.' Her name is Maxine. Does anyone know something about her?"

******

While I wrote personality features and followed mundane school board decisions in the early 1980s, a gruesome news story was unfolding all around us. The truth would not be understood until twenty years later. It was the case of the Green River Murders.

Young women began to disappear. Their bodies were discovered one by one around the area of the Green River, near the Enumclaw Plateau. King County police coined the name Green River Killer and assigned a task force to find him. The ultimate horror began to sink in when missing women and assumed runaways were numbered and their names and faces were posted among possible victims.

Dateline: Enumclaw

Could one killer have taken the lives of up to forty-two women?

The discovery of a body off Highway 410 past Enumclaw made us shudder. A killer had passed through our little city, taking the evidence of his crime past the stately homes on Griffin Avenue, past city hall, past Sunrise Pharmacy, past the Farman's Pickles plant, and up into the foothills of the Cascade Mountains.

Major coverage of the story was left to the dailies in the Seattle metropolitan area. As yet, no Enumclaw resident had been listed among the missing. My fellow reporters took the lead on hot news, especially when local search-and-rescue personnel became involved. I was a new mother by then and worked part-time hours. But I got out from behind my desk often and went to search for story ideas and photographs.

One summer day was too beautiful to remain inside. I took the prerogative of the news reporter and left my desk and the *C-H* staff behind me. My favorite destination on such a day was the country roads parallel to the main highway. The grid of narrow paved roads ran along the perimeters of the many dairy farms, where green pastures and golden buttercups still thrilled me. Against the brilliance of the blue sky, the ghostly and illusive Mt. Rainier played games with photographers. On this day, the 14,000-foot mountain was ours, a neat peak drawing my eyes to the perspective of the black and white Holsteins dotting the greenery. I

The Full Ripened Grain

loved the panorama from every angle, my camera ready at my side. I was joyful. I was heady and confident, having recently earned a third place for scenic photography from the Washington Newspaper Publishers Association.

As I guided my little green Mustang, turning left or right at the corners of each pasture, I became aware of a vehicle in my rearview mirror. It was a truck. A man was at the wheel. It was a little annoying having someone on my tail when I was trying to drive slowly, looking for photo opportunities. I turned left and he turned left. I turned right and he turned right. This was beginning to bug me when I decided to get his attention and wave him on around me. I slowed and tried to pull to the right, the deep ditches preventing me from leaving the road entirely. Watching the rearview mirror, I saw the driver shake his head back and forth, refusing the offer. He would not pass me? The shake of his head looked rather—sinister.

A terror began to rise from my insides, an inkling turning into a scalp-chilling realization that this guy could be the Green River Killer. And he was after me. There was no phone booth on the corner, much less a mobile telephone to call for help. I needed to get to someone—anyone. Only moments had passed when a white farmhouse came into view. I was familiar with the property. A pristine white fence surrounded milking barns. Immediately, I turned left into the driveway, ready

Dateline: Enumclaw

to jump out and rush to the front door. Looking into my rearview mirror, I watched in disbelief as the truck and its driver turned also and followed me into the driveway, blocking my exit. Leaving his truck, the driver approached my window. My window was closed. The door locked. I trembled.

"Hello!" he called and smiled. "Can I help you? My aunt lives here." The young man was on his way to visit his aunt and uncle and was in no rush. No need to pass on narrow roads.

My mind was racing as fast as my heart to grasp what was happening. I was embarrassed. Profoundly relieved and embarrassed.

"I…I'm from the *Courier-Herald*," I stammered. "I want to ask permission to take some photographs of this farm."

He was carefree and took three stairs at a time, hopping onto the porch as he called for his aunt. I was still taking shallow breaths when she emerged and I quickly refined my story. It was plausible. She happily agreed.

Legs shaking, I hoisted myself and my camera out of the car and staggered toward the fences lining the circular driveway. As I recall, the shots were a little out of focus.

*And we rejoice in the hope of the glory of God.
Not only so, but we also rejoice in our
    sufferings,
because we know that suffering produces
    perseverance;
perseverance, character; and character, hope.
And hope does not disappoint us, because God
has poured out his love into our hearts by the
    Holy Spirit,
whom he has given us.*

– Romans 5:2-5

MISSING MOM

I am cradled in her arms with my eyes shut tightly. The rocking motion becomes bothersome and I am slightly uncomfortable, even sore, from her firm embrace.

"Mommy, I'm asleep," I say.

"How can you be asleep when you are talking to me?" she responds, dryly.

The rocking continues.

It is my earliest recollection of Mother, this cozy image of a preschooler being rocked at nap time, the humorous exchange and irony in my mother's voice completely lost on me as a four-

Missing Mom

year-old. Now, it pleases me to have the tender scene locked in my memory banks. Less pleasing is the failure of this early attempt at communication between mother and daughter. To hide the truth, I said, "Mommy, I'm asleep." It never would have occurred to me to say, "Mommy, please stop rocking me now. I would rather lie down."

Even at the age of four, it seemed more important to put my feelings aside and humor her need to do the things she thought a good mother should do. I never would have intentionally hurt her feelings. I always thought complete honesty would have. I do not know where I got that idea, but the moment in that rocking chair symbolizes our entire relationship. We were close, but we usually failed to say precisely what we needed to say to one another.

When I need her now, and I do need her often, I try to conjure up the personality of the individual she was, rather than the loving and competent mother who met my most basic needs. The older I get, the more I regret having known only the mother she was and not enough of the woman she was. Women who have lived fifty years are sturdy pumps filled with knowledge just waiting to be primed. I could have learned a lot if I had just thought to ask.

My mother did not die, but the wonderful personality we knew and loved left our lives in May, 1976. My sisters and I watched helplessly as

The Full Ripened Grain

our 49-year-old mother, so pretty, petite and energetic, underwent a nightmare of surgery gone wrong. It resulted in permanent brain damage so severe that she remained in a persistent vegetative state (PVS) for the next twenty years.

The future had seemed bright for Mom as she found her way as a single career woman. I watched her thrive in the niche of the local business community of West Covina. She discovered leadership talent in herself which began to blossom. Her three girls were raised. She could turn her attention to her own life. Daughter Brenda married for the second time and we were happy for her and her daughter, Dawn, who was ten by then. Beverly married in 1969. She and her husband had a three-year-old daughter, Rhonda, and a new son, Ryan. With me married and at work in Washington, Mom's life was once again her own to pursue, and she succeeded. Mom worked in ready-to-wear fashion, supervising a chain of clothing stores that dotted shopping centers from Los Angeles to San Diego. She drove the freeways daily, where cities were spruced up for the nation's Bicentennial.

Mom was remarried, having lived a single mother's life since a humiliating split with our father. She surprised us all by eloping to Las Vegas. She had dated "George" on and off for four years. None of her family was there to witness the ceremony, which left us hurt and disappointed. We thought we should have been consulted. But she

Missing Mom

knew we were not pleased with her choice, even though she had accepted ours. Mom juggled her job, new marriage, and visits to children and grandchildren as best she could, with everyone vying for a piece of her time and attention.

She must have been exhausted. Worsening menopausal symptoms kept her feeling dragged out. Her doctor recommended a hysterectomy.

On the day of the surgery, I was comfortable staying in Washington, knowing that my sisters were with Mom at the hospital and would be close by for her recovery. I had had a satisfying visit with Mom and George at our home the week prior to her surgery.

We would learn the details of this medical catastrophe years later in court. But the effects were immediate. During the hysterectomy, the gynecologist performed a biopsy on a lesion he discovered on my mother's colon. He had not been given permission to do so. The procedure opened the door to infection that began festering the moment she was wheeled out of surgery. She woke up normally. Then began days of slow recovery. Nearly a week past the surgery, still hospitalized, my mother had a fever. Mom told me on the phone she was disappointed that she did not feel as well as she had hoped to by then. Her abdomen hurt. Tragically, she didn't complain. Our conversation on the phone would be our last.

News of a shocking phone call was waiting at the office of the *Courier-Herald* newspaper where

The Full Ripened Grain

I reported. I walked into the office, back from an assignment.

"Your two sisters have called," our bookkeeper told me. "One was crying. One wasn't."

My co-workers were quiet and attentive, scared for me as I dialed the hospital number left on the message pad. These people had just met my mother the previous week. My editor, Robert Olson, had greeted her warmly and enjoyed her southern accent and her vivacious reaction to our "pretty little city" of Enumclaw. I felt like an embarrassed teenager when she bragged about me. The whole office had listened and smiled at her charming delivery and my blushing face. This turnabout was unbelievable.

Mom's condition was grave. She had collapsed in her hospital room when her infected bowels burst. Emergency surgery was completed. Her heart stopped three times before she was revived and placed in intensive care.

She was alive. I raced to SeaTac Airport for the first available flight to Southern California.

Hurrying into the hospital that evening, I embraced my two stricken sisters. They were both in shock, mirroring my own expression. Everyone was hoping and no one was daring to think about losing Mom. Inside the intensive care unit, my mother lay pale and unconscious, surrounded by monitoring machines and tubing. The respirator pumped and hissed in a repetitive beat that imprinted itself in my memory. The acrid plastic smell of the room, the brown matter siphoned from my mother's abdomen assaulted me.

Late that night, we were still keeping vigil in the ICU, dazed by what we were facing. Mom's husband, George, was beside himself with anger and grief. He was beyond comforting. His new wife of only a year and a half was near death. Visitation was limited to one person at a time, so we took turns standing by her bed, talking to Mom in quivering voices, willing her to awaken and be okay.

Standing together, Brenda and Bill were both overwhelmed with concern. They had married seven months earlier in an intimate home wedding at Beverly's house. Twenty years her senior, Bill had hesitated to marry Brenda due to their age difference. But we liked Bill. He was roughly the same age as Mom, and the two became friends, allies in their love for Brenda and her little girl. All of us had been there and joyful. Now here we were, together again, this time in collective agony.

Bill felt a twinge in his chest and mentioned it to Brenda. But we were all upset, filled with sensations we had never experienced. Drained by the events of the day, we reluctantly left Mom in the nurses' care and went to Brenda's home to rest. We had a few hours of sleep before the world fell apart.

Brenda and I awoke very early. We had shared the king-sized bed at Bill's suggestion, while he took the couch in the living room.

The Full Ripened Grain

"You girls might want to talk," he said.

Remembering where I was, my hand flew to the telephone on the side table. I dialed the hospital. The nurse on duty was optimistic. She said Mom had made it through the night, although her condition was still critical. The message gave Brenda and me encouragement. We made a pot of coffee, then joined one another at the kitchen table feeling surprisingly calm, comforted by the familiar taste of the brew. Just a few feet away from us, Bill snored. We actually giggled at the noise, the humor being a welcome respite. Then the snoring stopped—abruptly.

Our tired minds took only seconds to realize something was wrong. We rushed to Bill. No response. We prodded. Still no response. There was a momentary flash when I thought he might be teasing us.

"Bill! Cut it out!"

Brenda staggered backwards, hand on her heart. "Call 911." She stood in shock before the wall phone in the kitchen as if she could not comprehend the numbers. I took the receiver and dialed the number, grateful for the woman's voice that answered immediately. In 1976, emergency systems needed more information from the caller and I tried my best. To my relief, I could recall the nearest cross streets after living away from the area for four years. Paramedics were on the way. They were so close by that we heard the siren the moment I hung up the phone. Neither of us knew

Missing Mom

CPR then, but Brenda tried to breathe into Bill's mouth as we had seen on television. The paramedics were in the driveway instantly and I waved them in. Brenda and I stood helpless, still in our bathrobes, as the men yanked Bill from the couch onto the firmer surface of the carpet.

They went to work on him with all their training. With their voices muffled, we heard whispered comments from the men to one another, but no one spoke to us directly. They prepared to transport him. We ran down the hall to dress quickly. We arrived at Queen of the Valley Hospital shortly after the aid car, and hurried across the threshold of the second hospital we were to visit that weekend.

That was the moment when I learned the difference between sad reality and films. There is no sound track to real drama. There is no silent pause. The sounds of people talking, crying and going about their business continue even when a doctor, who is a stranger, stands before you and tells you someone is dead. Looking at my sister, the man in the white coat addressed her.

"His eyes are fixed and dilated." He said.

What a strange choice of words, I remember thinking. I struggled for the meaning. But Brenda understood. Comprehension seeped into her face and I watched it contort into pain. The last sound we heard from Bill had been a massive heart attack from which no one could be revived.

The Full Ripened Grain

Our mother was clinging to life elsewhere, as far as we knew. We were needed there. But we were in a second crisis. Brenda sat down nearby, stunned and grieving, talking quietly to a priest who had arrived on the scene. I feared for my sister's mental state, wondering how much pain and loss one could survive all at once. Anguish made my gut hurt. How did Brenda feel?

I found a pay phone and called the first person I could think of—my father. Dad lived nearby in Downey. He was concerned about his former wife's condition and was waiting by the phone to hear from us. My call was brief and shocking. He was on his way. Then I called Beverly, who was at home with her toddlers, also waiting to hear word from us about Mom. I spoke as slowly and clearly as I could, relating the events of that early morning in such a way as to make sense to Dad and Beverly. None of it could possibly make sense.

It occurred to me that I did not know where my niece was. Someone had to tell her. Brenda told me Dawn was at the home of her friend Robin, who had agreed to take care of her overnight due to the crisis with our mother. This was the moment when I learned God leads us with help greater than the knowledge we have at hand.

Without directions or an address, I took Brenda's car and headed toward the neighborhood where I had a distant memory of once visiting Robin. I could not remember the exact house but I thought I would recognize it when I saw it. In a city of 100,000 people, in a neighborhood of cookie cutter homes and landscapes, I turned into the right driveway. I walked to the back door, stepped into the kitchen, and there was Dawn. Her face lit up when she saw me. My arrival was an unexpected surprise to them and they were happy to see me, so unaware of the sad news I brought with me. Dawn noticed my nervousness

"Why are you shaking?" she asked.

Robin waited as I took a deep breath and tried to settle my thoughts in some order. She thought she knew what I was about to say and seemed to steel herself.

"First of all," I said, placing my arm around Dawn's shoulder. She looked up at me, trusting and calm.

"Granny is still in the hospital and she made it through the night just fine."

Robin relaxed.

"But last night, Bill was very, very tired. This morning, he became very sick and had a heart attack. We called the fire department paramedics. They came as fast as they could. They worked very hard to help Bill. But Bill died."

Robin held onto the counter for support, groaning. Dawn burst into tears. I did too.

We held onto each other, not knowing what lay ahead of us. But for the moment, I was grateful to God for helping me find the right house and the right words.

*If you surrender completely to the moments as
 they pass,
you live more richly those moments.*

– Anne Morrow Lindbergh

MOTHER MOMENTS

Memories before and after the revelation of my parents' unhappiness and their separation subside as I recall happier times in girlhood when we are locked figuratively, in a child's sacred space marked "do not disturb."

We are on a vacation we could not afford if not for my Aunt Blanche and Uncle Charlie hosting us at a rambling two-story cabin at Priest Lake, Idaho. I have never seen such a beautiful, natural place. My mother is in her pretty one-piece bathing suit, standing on the dock jutting out over the gorgeous, sunlit lake. To me, she is Mommy as I have never seen her, so obviously fit and athletic, a side to her we never see at home. We have sat on a beach, but I don't think I have ever seen her swim. Our miniature poodle, Pierre, is by her side, as usual, so devoted to her. Mom is breathing deeply, taking in the pristine air when, without fanfare, she dives confidently, expertly, into the lake. *Wow*, I think.

Mother Moments

But suddenly, there is a wail, a racket at my side which is Pierre, frantic, hysterical, because he cannot follow my mother. He has never seen water deeper than a warm bathtub but I can see his loyalty overcoming his fear as he frets up and down the dock. He leaps into the chilly lake, coming up dogpaddling madly toward Mom, who is swimming toward a floating wooden raft. She pulls herself up the ladder and turns to see a black spot in the water trailing her. She laughs gaily and flattens herself on the raft where she pulls Pierre out of the water. He shakes fiercely and the spattered water sprinkles the air like my mother's laughter.

There are faraway glimpses of adult-like conversations between Mom and me. They seemed unimportant at the time but take on a new significance now because there were so few of them. I want to strain them with a sieve through my brain and collect them in an orderly file marked "Mother Moments."

I am a budding twelve-year-old and the buds are bigger than those of most twelve-year-olds. While seated at the kitchen table, Mom begins a casual conversation that seems pointless. With the fleeting attention span of an adolescent with tics, my mind begins to wander. And then I hear, "Oh, they'll tell you they will marry you, but don't believe them. That's what my mother always told me."

The Full Ripened Grain

Seeping into my consciousness is the fact that my mother has been talking to me about boys and how they might take advantage of me sexually and I HAVE NOT BEEN LISTENING. Whatever her mother told her has been passed on to the next generation and all my mental processes are focused on the fact that my tiny Alabama grandmother once talked about S-E-X and I haven't heard.

Mom interprets the astonished look on my face as awe, and she looks upon me tenderly.

I cannot bring myself to say, "How's that again?"

Mother confided in me one quiet moment when she felt I was old enough to handle some frankness.

"Your father and I have not been together as 'man and wife' in five years."

She was only 38 years old and attractive. But she told me she had a strict code of ethics. She was well-known and she had three girls to think about. At the time, I couldn't possibly appreciate her courage and sacrifice.

Finally, absurdly, Dad would use the threat of leaving again as punishment for his daughters when he was angry. He didn't realize how peaceful the house became when he was gone. This truth made me confused and guilty.

Of all the feelings associated with my mother from the part of her life we shared and the subsequent life endured in limbo, the least comfortable is anger. When Mom was newly divorced from my father and searching for a new life of her own, she left me unattended. I was fifteen by then and plenty old enough to be left alone. But not old enough to be left alone so much. I could have gotten in big trouble. Instead, I got straight As and abandoned my dating friends briefly for a more cloistered life. Dating that might lead to disastrous marriage seemed unappealing. So I was no trouble. No trouble at all. But I was angry, home alone after school and many weekend nights, resenting her for wanting to date. I was embarrassed by the whole idea of my mother going out with—MEN.

Waking on a Saturday morning, wearing my pajamas, with nothing planned but television, I walk to the kitchen and reach for a cereal bowl. I hear a sound from the living room. A man, a stranger to me, is sleeping on the couch. I run for my mother who is awake and so calm in reaction to my fright. It is only her date, she explains, who had too much to drink last night, so they agreed he should sleep on the couch for his safety. But what about my safety? Her safety? I never tell my father about this because I don't want him to know my mother had such a lapse in good judgment. He would hit the roof!

I wanted to say to her defiantly, "You don't have to take care of me. I'll take care of myself forever! You can count on it."

I have, too—with all the skills she taught me: the self-reliance I learned from her, the

The Full Ripened Grain

responsibility I accept daily because she raised me to do so, and the civic-mindedness she fostered by example. But there is practical training and there is emotional training. She gave me moments of both.

I am home from college for a weekend. Home is now a cookie cutter rental townhouse in West Covina, near Mom's work, the third place we have moved in three years. But home remains wherever my mother is. I have a frightening dream, a heart-pounding vision of a murderer stalking me on campus. I awaken and flee to my mother's room, for there is comfort and safety there. Mother is wakened and concerned. She takes the edge of the bedcovers and flings them open, an unspoken invitation to come to her. I am grown, acting so independent away at college, but this gesture is all I really need, not boyfriends or roommates or textbooks. I burrow into the covers and am her child again.

On my nineteenth birthday she escorts me to Las Vegas, a treat that includes my first ride on an airplane. The short flight from Southern California to Las Vegas is extravagant and goes by in a wink. She takes me to the Hilton, where Elvis Presley is headlining for the first time. We have good seats where waiters line up the two-drink minimum in front of me. To my amazement, Mother has told them it is my twenty-first birthday. I look so mature in my cocktail dress that I am not even carded. We watch The King captivate the audience and us. It is 1969 and Elvis is sexy and slim and a

Mother Moments

master showman. I am impressed with both Elvis and my mother. Who would think she could be so much fun at forty-two?

I was an unseasoned young woman in my twenties when Mom's life became suspended like the snow on a television screen after a moment's power failure. Unlike the television, however, there was no fixing it. By then, I had spent four years living twelve hundred miles away from her. There were phone calls and sweet letters, but no coffee dates or lunches where we could conspire and make that tenuous transition from mother and daughter to friends. The closest we came was a trip we made together with our husbands, just a week before that terrible day in May, 1976.

Mom brought her husband, George, to Seattle to spend a spring week with us. They had married in 1974. We decided to take them on a two-day trip to Victoria, British Columbia. We squeezed the two of them into the backseat of our Mustang, a spot one acquaintance called "the black hole." The trip became tiresome for all of us, but especially Mom, whose knee was hurting in the cramped bucket seat. She was stoic. After twenty-two years of marriage to my father, the "Gripe King," she rarely complained. When we got to our hotel, we dragged ourselves into the lobby and stood silently while our husbands registered. Quite in unison, the men turned to us and said, "Why don't you go get the luggage?" Mom

The Full Ripened Grain

grabbed the key dangled in our faces, and marched out of the lobby with me at her side.

"Humph!" Mom snorted. "If we weren't married, they would be falling all over themselves trying to get the luggage!"

It was only a moment, but it was one in which we became allied women. I wish there had been more of them.

But the time had grown short, without us knowing. She hugged me goodbye at the end of that week together, heading home for her planned surgery. I wasn't worried. She was only forty-nine, strong and vigorous. A hysterectomy was "routine."

Standing on our front porch on her way to the car, she turned to me and said, "I just wanted to come and see you. You know, I might not wake up."

Isn't everything you have and everything you are gifts from God? You already have all you need.

– 1 Corinthians 4:7-8

BEVERLY'S GIFT

It was my sister's final Christmas. Only forty-four, she was desperately ill with pancreatic cancer. I was on my way to be with her and her children early that December. I needed to be near her. But, I wondered, what gift could I bring when I knew it would be the last?

******

My niece Rhonda, shapely and strong at age twenty, climbed the aluminum extension ladder and secured strings of red, green and white lights to the eves of her house. I had never watched her do something like this before and I was impressed. Except for an assist here and there I provided, she was earnestly preparing Christmas all by herself. The little blue colonial-style house was old and unusual for this Covina neighborhood, filled with Southern California stucco. With the lights installed, it glowed like one of those sentimental Thomas Kincaid paintings. It made me feel sentimental.

To my knowledge, it was Rhonda's first time to do the task alone. This annual chore was something her mother usually did. As children of a single woman, Rhonda and her brother Ryan were used to watching their mother pound nails, hang fixtures and take care of tasks around the house herself. Now Rhonda was confident in every move, steadying herself on the edge of the ladder high above the front lawn. Her long glamorous fingernails and jangling bracelet seemed out of place, but she mastered the arc of the hammer as she worked.

Back inside the house, a six-foot sheared Douglas fir lay on its side, its heavy butt too large for the tree stand. After considering the task at hand, Rhonda grabbed a handsaw and set to work. I stood back, watching her elbow as it pumped back and forth, back and forth. Sifting sawdust filled the room with a lovely pine fragrance. Done. With my help, the tree was righted and inserted and tightened into the tree stand and shoved into the corner of the dining room. I returned to the kitchen and my pot of vegetable soup simmering on the stove. Rhonda turned her attention to a set of gigantic lollipops she intended to plant along the front walkway. The little blue house was ablaze with holiday cheer.

"Your mom will love this," I said.

Beverly's Gift

My sister, Beverly, had watched much of this decorating too. But she watched from the vantage point of the living room couch, where she lay covered by a blanket, too sick to get up.

"I'm so useless!" she sobbed. I rushed to reassure her.

With two children just on the verge of adulthood, she was dying. She had endured experimental procedures that kept her alive a miraculous thirteen months past the grim diagnosis. But after a year of valiant struggle, she was losing her life.

Since the diagnosis, I had told my husband and young children I would not sit twelve hundred miles away in Seattle and only wish I could be with her. The credit cards might be maxed out, but no matter how much it cost, I would see her as much as I could.

The concept of her death was unacceptable. To be separated from my sister, from the hazel eyes that laughed, from the ears that listened, from shared August birthday parties and revealing presents for each other at Christmas, from Beatle memories captured at a concert and a shared bedroom papered with John, Paul, George and Ringo, from bedspread-covered fears and our parents' strife, from hairspray overdoses and pantyhose wars, was beyond my grasp. No. It would not happen. Certainly not while we stayed this cheerful.

The Full Ripened Grain

I had arrived a couple days earlier from Seattle. I was met at LAX by my sister, Brenda, and her daughters Darcy, thirteen, and Crysta, twelve. It was a happy reception despite the Los Angeles rain. L.A. smelled good! Relieved to see each other, we hardly knew how to address the danger at hand. Our trio was threatened.

The "three Bs," our folks called us, and our father stuttered over our names like Porky Pig, lamenting, "Why didn't we call one of them Josephine!"

Dad had died in February. It had been only ten months earlier my husband and I and our children had driven here for my father's funeral. Not even one year had passed and now Beverly would leave us. Deeply frightened, Brenda and I were talking, moving, breathing, cleaning, going to work, cooking for our families. How was this possible? How could we function under such a threat? What could we do?

We made fudge. There was a culinary group hug in Beverly's kitchen the next day. I watched while Brenda and her girls set about this Christmas ritual, stirring the Kraft Marshmallow Crème into the melted chocolate chips, evaporated milk, butter, walnuts, and sugar. Beverly always made this recipe. This year we would just make it for her.

The back door opened and in came my niece Dawn. Brenda's eldest daughter lived only a backyard away from her Aunt Beverly and was a

Beverly's Gift

young mother. In her arms was four-year-old Jacklynn, who had visited her Great Aunt 'B' every day of her life. Crysta joked and did her best impression of Cher. While we spread the warm fudge in a pan, we all agreed that Crysta had serious talent. Beverly's son Ryan, seventeen, fled to the refuge of a neighbor's house as the feminine onslaught continued. We licked the spoon and scraped the boiler and talked about gifts, fattening recipes, and weight loss goals. Dawn and Rhonda modeled their new figures for me, each having lost forty pounds since I last saw them. It was a household of three generations of females pretending, just for the moment, that nothing terrifying was happening.

Twelve months earlier in January, Beverly and Ryan had come to visit my family in Washington State. We had the only boys in the family, and Ryan and my son, Evan, were due to go skiing together. But after their arrival, Beverly became too sick to go sightseeing. I wince now, thinking of my selfish disappointment. Beverly had cancer and we didn't know it. I thought only of how much I had yearned for her fun company, feeling lonely and isolated in a new community, hungry for the closeness of someone who knew me well. I soloed with the boys while she rested at our home with abdominal pain. We assumed it was the flu. Before they left at the end of the week, we cuddled on the front porch for a photo. There we are in the photograph, our arms around each other, smiling into the camera like two fools unaware of the disastrous wave looming behind us.

A month later, it is 4:00 p.m. on February 21, 1992 and the phone rings. A smothered voice, barely audible, says my name and "Dad's dead." It is Beverly, speaking as if someone has knocked the wind out of her. Our father has been killed in a car accident. The shock is not that he has died, for we have been threatened by his impending death for a long time. Following heart surgery at age sixty, he lived with severe heart disease for twelve years. The real shock is that this towering figure, this loved and resented parent, is truly gone. The moment has arrived and we all—I am certain of this—are caught between terror and relief.

"I had to see him," says Beverly. In convoluted fashion, she adds, "I had to make sure he was alright."

"Alright?" I question.

Beverly describes her arrival at the hospital where Brenda waits with Fred, Dad's partner of twenty-five years. Brenda was summoned by the hospital since Dad carried her name and number for emergencies. Beverly tells me how terrified she was that Daddy had been disfigured or mangled in some way.

"He looks normal," she says, "Except for being dead. Oh, and his shirt was torn by the

Beverly's Gift

paramedics who tried to revive him. One of his shoes is missing."

It is hard to explain how one can be grateful for this kind of detailed reporting.

Our mother said more than once, "Beverly has a memory like an elephant. She never forgets anything."

Weary from the twelve hundred mile drive to California, my husband Lynn, my children, and I walked slowly up to the doors of the funeral home, wearing our best. We had arrived in time for Daddy's viewing, that time when the family of the deceased has a somber "open house" in honor of their loved one. We didn't know who to expect.

Entering the mortuary, I saw Brenda and her daughters, so saddened by the loss of their only grandfather. The affection between them and their granddad had been very strong. The girls looked sweet in their best dresses.

As I entered the chapel, leaving my family behind me, Beverly intercepted me at the door and placed herself between me and the chapel aisle leading to Daddy's casket. She warned me, trying to soften the blow of his wretched appearance, but I had to—needed to—look.

The autopsy had left his body bruised. A crown of stitches circled his scalp. Some nameless medical examiner had cut my father's head open and put it back together. The mortician dyed his hair an unappealing reddish-brown to disguise it. It was nothing like the fine, graying light brown hair that was his. It was ghastly. I remained composed as a long line of earnest friends and colorful strangers filed through the chapel, offering their condolences to our catatonic faces.

After an hour of reunion and introductions, I sank into the front pew, drained by the experience. Beverly sat down next to me. We glanced at each other and then glanced into the family pews to one side of the casket. Behind a curtain, away from the eyes of the mourners stood Brenda, our sister in sorrow. She caught our eyes, raised her arms, clenched her fists and struck a pose. Moving sideways in a jerking fashion, she danced the Surfer Stomp into the ladies' room. Beverly and I were overcome with mirth. Our shoulders shook in our attempt to quell the laughter threatening to burst from our throats. We pursed our lips and gasped, confident that any visitors would come to the more logical conclusion that we were sobbing.

For the next few days, I was astounded by the fragile barriers which divide our emotions and our grief. And in such a short few months we were faced with it again. This time Beverly could not guard me from what I saw and felt.

The time came that Christmas when I had to leave Beverly. She was able to walk gingerly around the house and watched from a chair while the rest of us decorated the tree. I realized her

Beverly's Gift

collection of ornaments and knick-knacks was completely unknown to me. In all these years, had I never seen my own sister's Christmas collection? Nothing looked familiar. Not even Beverly. There was so much about her I still didn't know!

Before I flew home to my family and our own decorating, I helped Beverly teeter down the front steps of her house late one night. Center Street had quieted with no traffic passing by. Dressed only in our pajamas and robes, we stood together on the sidewalk in the California December chill and gazed upon Rhonda's work. It was a peaceful moment. Heavenly peace. With my arm around her shoulder, we took it all in and as I had said to Rhonda, she loved it.

"Merry Christmas!" she beamed.

It was still days before Christmas and I was back in my own home. The phone rang and it was Bev. She chatted and chattered, shivering due to a fever. I told her to go ahead and open the package I had left under her tree. My last gift to her was an ordinary electric blanket. Her last gift to me was that moment on the sidewalk.

He will yet fill your mouth with laughter and your lips with shouts of joy.

– Job 8:21

EATING GRIEF

Dad insisted on being buried in Meridian, a preference we had known for a long time. The distance narrowed our West Coast contingent to the three of us and Dad's partner, Fred, who stood with us at the Jackson airport window as Dad's casket made its way down a conveyor belt from the airplane to a waiting hearse. Fred drove to Meridian in a separate car, an arrangement we had not discussed. In our own rental car, our places were predetermined. Brenda took the driver's seat, Beverly took the front passenger seat, and I sat in the rear. I was quiet and gazed out the window at the familiar scenery. We were making a very personal pilgrimage to the city of our birth and didn't know what to expect. Did anyone remember Dad? Did anyone remember us?

We headed to Aunt Blanche's apartment where she welcomed us, tearfully. Also waiting were Dad's McGuffee cousins Betty, her sister, Marie, and husband Raymond, who would be a pallbearer.

Eating Grief

They were childhood playmates there to remember cousin Blake. They shared so many years and good times we really knew nothing about. At the funeral home, the doors to the visitation room opened and sixty people flooded in. There was a local radio announcement about the service the next day.

Faraway faces, from distant childhood recognition, made me feel transported back.

"You're the baby. I never met you," said one lady, taking my hand.

An elderly woman, Mrs. Snowden, introduced herself to me and told me she cared for my grandmother Letha Hudson when she died. She prepared her for burial. I was stunned by this reach across time, this woman connecting a son with his mother from her death in 1946. From across the room, a woman walked toward me, hands extended.

"You ARE Letha," she said, taking in my height, my face, and my figure.

Beverly met the family friend for whom she was named. I snapped a photo of the two. A toothless younger cousin told me he liked my dad because he taught him to play the piano. He did? He never taught me.

A contingent of old ladies arrived in support of my Aunt Fay. Dad's final visit to Meridian had been only five months earlier, in September. He played the piano for the residents of the retirement home where my aunt lived. He made new friends and fans.

The Full Ripened Grain

Amid the good wishes and sincere compliments about Dad's smile, personality and talent, I was so aware of surprise, a re-awakening or rediscovery of the charm that made Dad lovable. What a character he was! He saved his best for the public. He was, as Mom used to say, a street angel and a house devil.

The quiet service we expected turned into a full house of extended friends and family. There for us were my mother's relations from Demopolis, Alabama. Her brother, our Uncle Ronnie, came from Slidell, Louisiana.

Emotions erupted at the church. My Aunt Blanche wailed, hit hard by the loss of her big brother—it had been just the two of them growing up. My Aunt Fay cringed, not sure she could look at the casket, crying pitifully for her nephew. Only fourteen years older than him, she had been close to him, like an older sister. My aunts' grief weakened my composure and I wept softly along with my sisters. Somehow it seemed natural that we were reduced to just the three of us on the pew. No husbands, no children. It was what Dad missed most—just having us. Our families took our attention away from him.

A table laden with hot, hearty food awaited us when we walked into my aunt's apartment. The second funeral was over and my sisters and I led a solemn bunch of relatives, who were relative strangers, into the living room.

Eating Grief

Space was limited, but we all managed to find places to sit. A kind neighbor, also a stranger to me, removed aluminum foil from a deep roasting pan she hoisted from the oven. The aroma of Southern-style turkey dressing filled the tiny kitchen and my nostrils. It stirred a long-dormant memory of taste brought front and center in my brain, like memories of Dad only minutes before. It was him and Mom who introduced these dishes to me and cooked their version of them when we were transplanted to California as very young children.

I was grief-stricken and yet hungry. Who wouldn't be, when tantalized by an array of dishes that looked like Thanksgiving Day? The base of the dressing was baking powder biscuits which made it lighter, more like a soufflé than cornbread dressing. Lots of turkey broth, onion, celery, and beaten eggs baked the soupy mixture into a mellow side dish for slices of baked turkey, fried okra, tomatoes, and greens.

I marveled at this tradition of neighbors bringing prepared food to offer solace at the death of a loved one. It happens in every culture, though less in ours as we maintain distance from our neighbors. We build gourmet kitchens and cook less. The gesture of bringing nourishment makes the giver feel less helpless, as we all feel when friends lose someone dear to them. The food is tangible caring. Loving kindness is part of the recipe.

The Full Ripened Grain

And then there was dessert. A caramel cake, three layers of golden cake standing tall and perfect. It was smeared with icing the color of brown sugar in between the layers and over the top—like the taste. So fresh! So lovingly homemade. We consoled ourselves with the sweet taste following some bitter tears.

The warmth of the turkey and dressing on this clear winter day in February seemed to have a good effect on everyone. What began next was unexpected group therapy. Aunt Blanche, Cousin Letha (named for our grandmother), Cousin Betty, Marie and Raymond, Brenda, Bev, Fred and I all recollected the funny and sad, irritating and endearing characteristics of my father. He drove us mad. Fred mostly watched, listened and chuckled.

"I'm having such a good time!" he said, taking it all in.

He did not offer any stories, although he had spent more time in recent years with Dad than anyone else.

A week prior, I never would have dreamed I would be in Meridian, Mississippi that day. And yet the sudden immersion in Southern style was an invigorating change. I sat transfixed while my Southern cousins from New Orleans and Meridian entertained me with their outspoken drawls. They debated all the hot topics, including the merits of raising kids with spanking, which was what they all experienced.

Eating Grief

"I tell you it was child abuse!" Cousin Betty said.

"They did it because they LOVED us," Cousin Raymond said.

The 1992 rape trial of boxer Mike Tyson was in the news.

"He is guilty, guilty, GUILTY," said Aunt Blanche, brandishing a cigarette between her fingers. Tobacco smoke swirled around the apartment. No one even asked.

"You...ah...full...of... s-h-i-t," said Cousin Marie, too refined to say the word.

"God damned bastards!" Aunt Blanche retorted, fiery in her declarations.

Profanity-laced conversation of the most ferocious kind was volleyed about in what turned out to be good-natured banter. When she escorted them out the door with hugs, Aunt Blanche turned, leaned her head back against the door and said, "I just LOVE Raymond and Marie."

I shook with laughter, the competing personalities conjuring up visions of my Dad and how he might have jumped in. He would have eaten hearty and he would have laughed hearty.

*The spirit of a person will
sustain him in sickness,
But who can bear a broken spirit?*

– Proverbs 18:14

PRACTICAL MATTERS

Brenda and I agreed sadly that it was a blessing Dad had gone before Beverly, because her cancer would have caused more pain for him than we could imagine. As for Brenda, she became Beverly's health advocate. It was an aching concern separate from the sad vigil she kept for Mom, who still remained bedridden and unresponsive after seventeen years. Beverly's early symptoms and efforts to find a cause were unsuccessful. Brenda wanted answers NOW. She would rage at me over the phone, fuming at the doctors.

"The damned HMO is so slow. Her eyes are yellow! They make her an appointment in six weeks, she finally goes, then waits two weeks for the results."

We thought our sister might have hepatitis.

Practical Matters

By the time Beverly was hospitalized the first time, she was actually close to death from cancer.

The phone rings at my house on a day in April 1992, when contractors are working upstairs on a room addition. The grief over our father's death in February has abated somewhat and I am showing interest in my home. Outside, the yellow forsythia has opened in my neighbor's garden and daffodils line the roadways while the trees are still stark. It is the annual promise of spring in the Northwest. A green haze of buds and Neapolitan ice cream-colored fruit trees announce that we are waking again.

I answer the phone and it is Brenda, reporting in.

Beverly is stuck in a hospital in downtown Los Angeles with a doctor who is searching for answers. Her urine is black.

"The doctor says he thinks 'we may just be able to keep her comfortable!'" Brenda whispers.

"WHAT?" I answer, hardly able to comprehend what Brenda is telling me.

All signs point to liver cancer. The source is unknown.

"We just lost Dad. This can't be happening."

We talk. Brenda's business needs her. Beverly needs her. I arrange to stay at the hospital to help both my sisters.

When the phone is settled back in its cradle, I sob, tears loud enough for the contractor upstairs to hear.

He looks at me over the bannister. I look up, quieted. I speak the unspeakable.

The Full Ripened Grain

"My sister has liver cancer."

"Do you want me to call your husband?" he asks kindly.

***

The burial of our father becomes a fast memory as we move forward to help Beverly. We were sure we would grow old together, like our great aunts before us. Instead we are on the phone to them in Mississippi with the startling news that Beverly is seriously ill. I hear the tears in their voices.

Brenda tells me this:

She is standing in the hospital room next to Beverly, who is sitting up in bed. Beverly's children, sixteen and nineteen, are in school, waiting like all her friends and co-workers to hear news of the doctors' findings.

An oncologist enters the room with the news. Somberly, he relates the results of the latest tests. The diagnosis is metastasized liver cancer. The source of the cancer is unknown, but there could be a pancreatic tumor.

Unknown to the oncologist is that Beverly has just thoroughly enjoyed watching the film *Kindergarten Cop*, in which burly star Arnold Schwarzenegger confronts an annoying student.

"I have a headache," says Arnold.

"Maybe it's a tumor," says the nasty boy.

"IT'S NOT A TOOMAH," says Arnold.

Practical Matters

At this message from the doctor, Beverly looks up at Brenda and in her very best Arnold Schwarzenegger impression, she says, "It's NOT a toomah!"

Brenda laughs heartily. We are always each other's best audience.

Stunned, the doctor looks at the floor, takes off his glasses and says, "In all my years of practice, I have never had such news greeted with such humor."

Beverly calls to tell me herself. "It's an 'M' word," she says.

I reply cautiously, "Metastasized?"

"Yes, that's it."

And so it was Beverly's case that sparked creativity in the department of gastroenterology. Using a scope to find the tumor, they also decided to insert a stent in her malfunctioning liver. The bile cleared and Beverly's color returned to normal. Not only that, she returned to work. The doctors marveled at her transformation.

Brenda wasn't so sure.

"She doesn't seem to be angry about it," she tells me. "I don't think she is fighting."

An old conversation between Beverly and me surfaces in my memory. She told me of the time she was attending adult Sunday school at her church while briefly living in Kentucky. The teacher asked if God told them they only had a few months to live, how would they feel?

Beverly raised her hand.

The Full Ripened Grain

"Relieved," she said.

The conversation haunts me.

Her body rejects the liver stent, fever raging, so the doctors do it again. She is well enough to fly north to visit with me and Lynn and the kids. We shop a little, meet my girlfriends. I am so happy to pamper her, to cook for her.

Weeks pass. Back in West Covina, Brenda and I take her to Brenda's house to discuss some matters. I glance into the family room where Beverly has already fallen asleep in a recliner. We gaze affectionately at her, then we gaze at each other, both numbed with dread.

On a day closer to the end, Beverly tells us she needs help with her bills, a foggy awareness of her responsibilities making it through the pain meds. Brenda has already assumed control as she did with Dad's paperwork. I am fine with this, as it has always been easy for me to give up authority to my older sister. Beverly's leased car is returned with no problem. Creditors are surprisingly gracious. It is tedious but important business and Brenda assures Beverly she does not have to worry.

There is a knock at the door of Beverly's house the week before she dies. Brenda and I open it and there stands a saleswoman selling—of all things—cemetery plots. She comes with literature, apologizing up front if she has inadvertently come to a house where there is illness. We are cool about it as Beverly is actually out of bed and puttering in the kitchen behind us.

Practical Matters

But we are listening.

Like tiny planned condos, the lovely cemetery nearby has plots open in a newly developed section. They are available at bargain rates if you get in on it. Practical to the core, Brenda and I take the literature and give the lady "the eyeball." We know Beverly has a life insurance policy with her job, but knowing the cost of our father's services, we feel duty-bound to save our niece and nephew some money.

An appointment is made and the next day, the two of us leave Beverly with a hospice nurse and walk to a nearby building where the saleslady has a temporary office upstairs.

Hesitantly climbing the steps, we are frankly shocked at each other.

"How can you do this?"

"What do you mean? You're doing it too."

"Is this legit? How do we know she isn't a fraud?"

"Does this mean we are giving up hope?"

"Can we sign for Beverly? How much should we spend?"

Feeling like ghoulish rag ladies from a Charles Dickens story, we guiltily fill out the forms to buy a plot in one of the nicest memorial parks in the valley.

"It's a kindness really," we agree. We are just putting our recent experience to good use as the loving aunts and sisters we are.

Three years later, we will bury Mom there too.

*Love never gives up, never loses faith,
is always hopeful, and endures through every
circumstance. Love will last forever.*

– 1 Corinthians 13:7-8

WAKING FROM THE AMERICAN DREAM

"This is like Cinderella," says my sister.

Like my very own fairy godmother, Beverly is standing in my living room with her arm raised in the air as if she is holding a wand. Her comment is meant to compliment our new house, but I can sense the bewilderment behind her happy expression. It is me, her baby sister, the girl who went to college and wanted a career, who owns Beverly's American Dream.

It is 1991. I have one terrific husband, three kids, a station wagon, a nicely furnished house and a beagle. I have no salaried job, but a busy life filled with family and volunteerism in our new home on Bainbridge Island, Washington. Without bitterness, Beverly nudges me to understand the privilege and preciousness of my stay-at-home mother life.

Waking from The American Dream

We have heard in the news, more and more, about how American families are changing and dependent on double incomes. The need for quality daycare is a national topic and a huge expense for the families with both moms and dads in the workplace. Our expenses are growing too, but Lynn's salary and the annual interest I receive from my mother's trust allow me choices. I can work at a paid job and spend a lot of that money on daycare, or I can take care of my own children. I like being the main caregiver for my children. When I explain this to Mom's husband, he tells me, "Wouldn't that make your mother happy?" We agree.

Beverly married her high school sweetheart in 1969, but the dream faded quickly. Beverly wanted to be a stay-at-home mother. She wanted to populate a backyard with neighborhood kids. She wanted to fill a wading pool and make Kool-Aid in the summer. She wanted to go to Little League games and dance recitals. She had earned her own money, having had a part-time job since she was sixteen. After working the first three years of her marriage, she stayed home with their first baby. But they had a mortgage and a new car and stretched themselves too far financially. The pressure was on.

Dad chastised them, critical of their financial decisions. "They want everything we have worked all our lives to own!"

The Full Ripened Grain

Their daughter was born in 1972, then a son in 1975. She left a bookkeeping job and stayed home to take care of them, with expectations of support by her husband. She loved her home life with her children and shared it with their friends, Mom and Dad, and all of us on different occasions. Mom and Dad were adoring grandparents. But things weren't going well with Beverly's marriage. Holding three-year-old Rhonda and six-week-old Ryan, Beverly sat down on the front steps of their home in Covina and tried to explain one day, why daddy would not be coming home that night. Beverly was still recovering from a C-section. She could not even look for a job yet. Beverly found herself begging for reconciliation with her husband. Denied.

After the first awful months following their split, Beverly managed to get a job as a bookkeeper and paid for babysitters, some good, some bad. Her ex-husband paid his child support faithfully. The amount remained the same for years, even though the children and their expenses got bigger and his income increased. So Beverly went to court to ask for the amount to be raised. She won.

Still, there was never enough money to live the way she wanted to live. She wanted to provide the good things for her children like new clothes, music lessons, a clean decent house, and enough food, heat, telephones, television and trips to the movies. She wasn't expecting posh vacations. She just didn't want her failed marriage to deprive her children of the American lifestyle she desperately wanted them to have. She wanted to give them all the basics our parents had provided, and some of the extras they hadn't.

Beverly wasn't alone in those desires. At the same time nationally, women fought for equal pay and supported an Equal Rights Amendment that was never ratified. Beverly was one of millions of women holding responsible office jobs that paid a stagnant full-time salary of about a thousand dollars a month, gross.

At that same time, I was ensconced in a two-career marriage with no children yet. I had no idea what it was like to get two children fed, dressed and out of the house to day care and report to work on time. Being twelve hundred miles away, I had little to offer other than a sympathetic ear, a little loan now and then, and a place to visit for the holidays.

At the end of one such visit, we are standing at SeaTac Airport saying goodbye. We are killing time before Beverly's departure by browsing around a gift shop in the terminal. Beverly chooses a ring from the case and tries it on her finger. It is not expensive, a mere fifteen-dollar bauble of costume jewelry. She decides to buy it and takes out her credit card, a card I know is almost past its limit.

Here she goes again, I think. Much of our personal conversation has centered on her budget problems. I think this purchase is idiotic. I express

The Full Ripened Grain

my disapproval by saying what I think is a tactful rebuke.

"Oh Bev, you don't need that."

But a rebuke is a rebuke and she buys the ring defiantly, ignoring my comment with stony silence. Only later she gets up the nerve to jab back.

"I'll buy a ring if I want to!"

It is as close as she has ever come to saying, "Mind your own damned business."

Beverly explained her point of view to me before, but I had forgotten.

It seemed our mother had explained the identical feelings to Beverly and Beverly had concurred.

After their divorces, they felt ugly and unwanted, like no one would ever find them attractive again. Both had suffered excruciating rejection. Though they felt powerless, at least they had the power over how to spend their small incomes. And so they pampered themselves when they could with their credit cards, which became symbols of independence and power for them. They ultimately bought sleepless nights and humiliation when they had to ask for family loans to cover their debts. For us who worked hard at living within our means, it was difficult to be gracious about handing over a hunk of modest savings without feeling as if we had deprived ourselves for someone else's rainy day. It wasn't fair and she knew how I felt.

Waking from The American Dream

But it was not fair that she was the one living single and trying to make it on one small salary with two children. I felt guilty about my disapproval of Beverly's spending habits and I tried to make up for it by defending her to our father, who had only criticism and no money to offer. Brenda came to Beverly's rescue on a regular basis, with large sums of cash—some paid back, some not.

On a spring day in 1985, ten years into her single parenthood, my phone rang. It was Beverly, sobbing. "What am I going to do?" she begged, the tremble in her voice sounding so alarming. I listened.

Her rental home had been sold. She was evicted and did not have the thousands of dollars it would take to pay for first and last month's rent, cleaning and utility deposits for yet another overpriced Southern California dwelling. She had two years of college, earned before her marriage, and a full-time office job at a fuel transport business. But it was not enough to save her from her situation.

In desperation, she reluctantly surrendered her young teenagers to their father. It was the ultimate disgrace, an unbearable defeat. Our mother had been an invalid for ten years by then and could not help. It was our dad who offered shelter. For the next six months she lived with our father and his partner, Fred, who welcomed her. Despite sympathy and hot breakfast lovingly forced upon

The Full Ripened Grain

her in the morning, her situation sent her into psychotherapy.

At thirty-eight, she was a child come home to an ancient relationship fraught with mental conflicts and resentments. When she was alone, she called me collect to get the "crap" off her chest, as she said. Years later, I cannot remember a single thing I said that might have soothed her agony at losing her independence. Did I listen well? What did I say? Did it help her?

Beverly's tears fell in sharp contrast to her social reputation as a clown. She even owned a collection of clown dolls, paintings, and figurines that adorned her living room. She cultivated her reputation through high school and at regular reunions of her class of 1966. It was Beverly who performed as master of ceremonies to the delight of her fellow alumni. She could be hilarious. In private, she could also be catty and viciously sarcastic. She was like a wounded animal who could be grateful for affection, or turn and bite.

Beverly fought to keep her weight down and hated the "jolly fat woman" image on her five-foot, three-inch frame. She practically coined the phrase "yo-yo syndrome" with her regular journeys up and down the bathroom scale. She stayed impeccably groomed with short haircut, makeup, nails, and clothes that were always current. She had fair skin and a round face that tanned easily, hazel eyes, and a brilliant smile. Her self-esteem was in the toilet.

"Who would want a fat lady with two kids?" she said.

I protested, but I knew the hurt behind the poor self-image, the damage too deep to recover. She was the child in the middle, never fully celebrated. She ate to fill a hunger that could not be satisfied. She wanted and deserved to be cherished.

It was a fact she was cherished by many people, but never the lover she fantasized. She was everybody's favorite friend. Beverly was great company. I should know. She was my first playmate.

Stuck in the middle, she was born two years after big sister and two years before me, an arrival which disturbed her status as the new kid on the block. Our parents said "she started crying and never stopped." It was pretty standard Dr. Spock baby psychology. Mom had to keep her from pinching me between the slats of my crib. I have a tiny scar on my right thumb where Beverly burned me with the car cigarette lighter. In return for her animosity, I gave her my adoration, following her everywhere and calling out "Dab-a-doh," my toddler version of her multi-syllabic name.

By virtue of her superior status as the eldest, Brenda was given her own room whenever our parade of rental houses contained more than two bedrooms. By default, Beverly and I became perpetual roommates, with side-by-side twin beds, perfect for talking and listening to our parents argue. On one particular night, I can remember an argument coming to a close. Mom and Dad each walked separately into our room. Each kissed Bev, then tucked her in. Each turned and kissed me and tucked me in. Like a dutiful assembly line, they tried to make us feel secure. I think they were trying to make themselves feel secure.

As a teenager, Beverly was a hairspray-squandering, stocking-stealing slob. But she and her friends were decent to me, including me in a lot of their chatter during wall-to-wall slumber parties. In 1964 we plastered our room with Beatles posters and dreamed of meeting them. I grieved and resented it when she and her friends got tickets to see the Beatles in concert at the Hollywood Bowl and left me out, but I shared her obsession. I bragged about her nerve. A day after the concert, she and her friends heard on the radio that the Beatles were attending a garden party in Beverly Hills. They found their way from West Covina to Beverly Hills, talking their way past a security guard at a roadblock in one neighborhood. Hearing party sounds, her friends hoisted Beverly up to see over a tall hedge. John Lennon was standing in the distance, facing the hedge with a drink in his hand. He waved. Mission accomplished. A lifetime coup.

In her struggle to find another home, Beverly watched the daily progress of an old house undergoing remodeling. She fantasized about it, watching the modest little two-story colonial-style house take shape day to day on her way to work. The rent was more than she could afford, but it was the kind of place she had dreamed about, a house with character and a fenced yard—room enough for her children and a dog too. She stopped one morning and sat on the front step until the owner arrived. She declared her intentions. She moved in on borrowed money and created a cozy home for herself as well as Rhonda and Ryan. A happy result of the eviction crisis was that they became closer to their father, who lived a short distance away from the new rental. Things were looking up.

Beverly took a leap of faith and took an exam to become an emergency telephone operator for the Baldwin Park Police Department. As a woman aged forty, public employment statutes now placed her in a "protected class" of workers and her age became an advantage. She went through a battery of tests and an investigation by the department that included thorough background checks and statements from me and other people who knew her.

I told them about the time Beverly was at the home of her high school girlfriend, Rita, who went into childbirth labor during the casual visit. They had not seen each other for quite some time. No matter. With Rita's husband away from the house and nowhere to be found, it was Beverly who got her friend to the hospital. Not only did she stay by Rita's side, she was able to fill out the hospital forms, her keen mind pulling up long-remembered details of her friend's birthdate and next of kin and their addresses.

The Full Ripened Grain

"Oh Beverly!" Rita said. "I can't remember my OWN name right now!"

When Rita's husband finally appeared, someone had to be excused from the delivery room. The nurses were sorry to see Beverly go.

She got the job! Beverly began training that placed her in the operations section of the police department, with a new schedule of graveyard shifts and 911 emergencies. She had fascinating work and the greatest advantage was a retirement policy and HMO benefits to protect herself.

When she could afford to, she started classes to complete her college degree. She used my adulthood diagnosis of Tourette syndrome as a subject for a paper in her psychology class. I was happy to cooperate and even learned more through her research. It was wonderful for me to watch her dream and succeed and finally realize how bright she was. Her counseling seemed to have helped a great deal. Dad had a big place in her life, but she was her own woman now, not an embarrassed teenager.

Our mother was well at the time of Beverly's first separation and only the two of them know what wisdom passed between them. By the time the marriage ended and she was so in need of her mother's help and counsel, the long vigil for our mother had begun. Beverly waited seventeen years to learn the outcome of Mom's condition. Who would ever have thought Beverly would die first?

Waking from The American Dream

Beverly had health problems before the big one. Overweight and eating too much sugar and fat, Beverly had a gall bladder attack in 1990. An operation removed it. She flew north for a visit with me during her recovery. She told me that when she woke up in the hospital, she saw a figure sitting still in the corner of the room. It was Dad. He had been nervously waiting for her to awaken. Our mother's circumstances had taught us all to beware of "routine" surgery. We would never take these procedures for granted again.

At the end of her life, Beverly got the love and attention she needed and then some. Affection for Beverly ignited a sense of family and brotherhood in the Baldwin Park Police Department when news of her pancreatic cancer surfaced. Beverly had miraculously returned to work following her first treatments. I have often wondered if during those few weeks, her actions may have saved a life. I like to think God rewarded her courage. Officers shepherded our family as Beverly's death approached. A high school friend and officer, Larry, kept tabs on us all. As a department, they were ready to help.

A network of police officers, friends and family stood watch at Beverly's house until her death on March 4, 1993. On the day of her funeral service, I stood, agog, when lights from a long line of police cars, lights flashing, filed into Oakdale Cemetery. It would make the newspapers that day, an entire city police department taking time to honor Mrs.

The Full Ripened Grain

Beverly Long. And that a neighboring city, West Covina, took their emergency calls for the duration of Beverly's funeral. Officers in full uniform, hands gloved in white, upheld her casket as pallbearers.

At her service, my mind strays into regrets: It is the day before her wedding in April, 1969, and she is furious with me because I cannot sing. She is trying to stay calm but the pressure is getting to her, the wedding preparations having become overwhelming. I am sick. Not too sick to cancel my role as a bridesmaid, but too sick to sing. My throat is raspy and my voice nearly gone. I let her down on one of the most important days of her life. But then, just a year ago, she asks if I will sing at our father's funeral. Yes, yes, I tell her. I think I can do it. I sing well and make her proud of me. Twenty-three years to make amends? What else have I left undone?

Now it is her funeral and I cannot possibly muster the strength and spirit to sing, not even to honor her. A stranger sings for me—"Over the Rainbow"—and I am reminded of Beverly's fondness for the Wizard of Oz, who tells the Tin Man, "A heart is not judged by how much you love, but how much you are loved by others."

There were dear faces in the crowd, but I was unable to speak, acknowledging them with a pathetic, inadequate glance. In the chapel the police chief acknowledged her service to the department, raising his hand-held radio to the microphone for us to hear a final broadcast dispatch in her honor. The entourage of earnest policemen escorted her casket to the graveside where each pallbearer tenderly laid a white pair of gloves on the floral spray.

When all of us stepped into the spring sunlight, the entire Baldwin Park Police Department stood in formation at attention on the lawn facing the chapel. Brenda and I sought each other's reddened eyes and found our voices long enough to whisper that we found it unimaginable that such a show of honor and respect would ever be displayed for us. This middle child had trumped us. Sibling rivalry to the end.

*Because of Christ and our faith in him,
we can now come fearlessly into God's presence,
assured of his glad welcome.*

– Ephesians 3:12

MOM'S FAREWELL

On January 11, 1996 Brenda called to tell me our mother was at the brink of death. Come, she said.

After nearly twenty years of waiting for the other shoe to drop, I didn't want her to die without us there. New grief, new tears flowed. My eight-year-old, Kirk, saw my tears and cried for me. As I tucked him into bed that night, he cried again because he had not met her. He amazed me with his sensitivity and empathy for me. Eden, thirteen, said she too, was sad for me and for herself because she had never met her grandmother. At age ten, she traveled with me to see Aunt Beverly. As it turned out, she bravely flew home by herself because Beverly's cancer had advanced too much and I needed to stay longer. With her aunt's condition being so severe, I hadn't the heart to take her to meet her invalid grandmother. Had I made a

Mom's Farewell

big mistake shielding the children from the sad lady in the bed?

I thought that since they could not meet their "real" granny, I didn't want them to see what was left of her when, in fact, a visit to her might have helped them understand this tragedy and why it saddened me so. My three children attended my father's funeral in California years earlier. Although they were so young, they seemed to understand it was a time to be together and they took their cues from us. But of course, they knew their granddaddy.

At Brenda's call I flew to Los Angeles. I sat in the hospital room with Mom for a couple hours each day for a week. Mom appeared unchanged, although it was strange to see her away from her private house with the sunny bedroom. I watched the private nurses care for her, gently. We talked as they took Mom's vital signs. Mary Jane, Lily, Pat, Monica. How do they do it, I wondered, utterly grateful for their skill in caring for a patient for so many years. Mom's blood pressure dipped dangerously low, perhaps signaling her body's cessation of life. I noticed that the doctors rarely came by. I understood. None of them wanted to do anything that might prolong her life, or, heaven forbid, be the one responsible for ending it.

Mom turned sixty-nine that month. I kissed her, but left for home without saying the usual tearful farewell. I was tired of goodbyes. She was discharged a few days later, alive.

The Full Ripened Grain

Five months later, Brenda called again. The twentieth anniversary of Mom's tragedy approached and we agreed we should do something to mark the occasion. It was the anniversary of Bill's death too. But Brenda's remarriage, two years after Bill's death, had endured with the birth of two daughters. Their childhoods were marked by regular visits to their invalid grandmother's house where they played while their mother visited with the nurses and Mom.

Twenty years! We never heard her voice again. We never got a letter, a phone call, a gift, advice, word of encouragement, company, comfort, a smile, a hug or help when our babies were born. No mothering, ever again. No love. No sharing. I wanted her to see my babies. I wanted her to hold them and see how beautiful and how smart they were. We had no closure of a funeral. Just waiting.

We wait a little every day. We wait for the beep. We wait for the bus. We wait for our meal. We wait for the doctor. We wait for our kids while they have a lesson or a dental appointment. We wait for the light to change. We wait for the elevator to come. Almost every time we wait, we know the waiting will be over soon. And still we become impatient! How do we handle waiting when the waiting is too long?

How do we wait for years? We pray and the answer is not "yes" or "no." It seems to be "Just wait."

Mom's Farewell

Halfway through my agonizing wait I spent a weekend at a Christian conference, listening to a wise woman speak. Her name was Ruth and she told us the story of how she was training a Saint Bernard. She took her dog to a sandy hill and gave him the "sit-stay" command. She got in her car and began to back away. The anxious dog stayed and waited. Finally she stopped the car and called to him. Relieved, the dog ran to her in a frenzy of love and gratitude. Friends asked her how she could be so cruel. Cruel? She told them she knew all along what she had planned for him. Then I felt as if she were speaking to me directly.

"Have you ever felt as if God has stranded you on a hill and abandoned you?"

Yes, Yes, I thought. All the time. And then she said something I will always remember.

"What God does in us as we wait, is as important as what we are waiting for."

I could only trust that God had a plan and so I waited.

Then on May 18, 1996, Brenda invited all of the nurses who attended Mom over the years to come for lunch. Mom was dressed in her best nightgown and pretty sheets. The nurses marveled at how she endured. There were fifteen nurses there, all happy to see each other and Mom. Our timing was perfect. Just a month later she was gone.

Even after twenty years and one month, her death came as another crisis and I relived the

The Full Ripened Grain

sorrow of her loss. She was once again in the hospital. Brenda called. The feeding tube in her abdomen was infected and there was internal bleeding. Her blood pressure was dropping. There was a "Do Not Resuscitate" order. Brenda drove as fast as she could, but missed Mom's passing by ten minutes. She told me she was waiting for the doctor to pronounce death. There was no heartbeat, no pulse. Mom was just gone.

On June 24, 1996, I wrote in my journal:

"I was angry at God last night and went to bed telling him off. I would not go, I would not. Cruelty. I accused Him of cruelty—both for Mom and us. I prayed in church for her when they got to the part about praying for those who suffer—like I have every Sunday for twenty years. Still, I felt hit in the stomach unprepared for the finality. It will be a change of life for me. Especially Brenda."

We placed an obituary in the *San Gabriel Tribune* so that people who knew and worked with Mom might see it. Did anyone remember her?

Once again, our whole family packed our bags for a sad trip. The night before our flight, I was overwhelmed by sadness. It was time to say a final goodbye. How could I be reluctant? I had so much time to prepare yet I was nervous, dreading the moment.

The next day was the funeral. A minister we did not know took time to meet with all of us and talked to us about our individual relationships with our mother. He knew about our long wait.

Mom's Farewell

We did not speak about the sad parts of her life, the split with our father. The emphasis was on the mother and woman she was. Many of Brenda's friends were there as well as George, who remained Mom's husband and trustee. Over the years, he made a life for himself in San Diego with his son and family from his first marriage. Beverly's children were there too, taking time to visit her grave a few yards away.

We gathered at a graveside service, her casket covered in yellow roses. The day was better than sunny. It was a perfect 75 degrees, breezy and comfortable. There were about thirty people there, including seven devoted nurses. How could I truly thank them? One of them was Heidi, who was just twenty-two when she came to take care of my mother. She stayed for eighteen and one half years. She had two children, now ten and eight, and lived her whole married adult life as Mom's night nurse.

I sang "I Asked the Lord." My voice felt strong and I loved its message:

> *I asked the Lord to comfort me,*
> *when things weren't going my way.*
> *He said to me, "I will comfort you and lift*
> *your cares away."*
>
> *I asked the Lord to walk with me*
> *When darkness was all that I knew*
> *He said to me "Never be afraid for*
> *I will see you through."*

The Full Ripened Grain

And then the pastor took over. He read a passage in the Bible we talked about earlier, the one I read a zillion times over twenty years because it spoke to me about Mom. It is the part in Romans 5 where it says we stand in grace by faith and rejoice in hope of the glory of God. And not only *that*, but we also rejoice in our struggles, knowing that to struggle and overcome produces perseverance; and perseverance, character; and character, hope.

The pastor read quotations from all of us about Mom and there was some laughter too. Brenda told how Mom was angry one night because teenaged Brenda and her friend, Robin, who grieved with us, were very late and hadn't called. While pacing the floor, Mom heard them drive up and looked out the window. She saw Robin get out of the car to lift the garage door for Brenda. In the darkness and spotlight glare of the headlights, Robin bent over to grab the handle of the door and flung her skirt up over her head, baring her petticoat and underwear to the world. Mom cracked up. She could never stay mad at any of us.

And of course, there was Psalm 23 when we read that she would "dwell in the house of the Lord forever." Unlike the first funeral of my youth, I could feel certain. Yes, FOREVER.

When he asked if anyone else had something to share, my eight-year-old Kirk raised his hand. I held my breath. The pastor called on him.

Mom's Farewell

"You know," said Kirk. "I'm sort of glad she died because now she doesn't have to be sick anymore and can be with God."

The pastor said he thought a lot of us might be thinking the same thing.

*Encourage one another daily; as long as it is
   Today...
We have come to share in Christ if we hold
   firmly
till the end of the confidence we had at first.*

– Hebrews 3:13-14

MARCH RERUNS

Today is the fifteenth anniversary of Beverly's death and I miss her. I shuffle through drawers of photographs and find Kodak Brownie snapshots of her smiling at me. I see us holding hands in our Easter dresses and Halloween costumes or cheek to cheek in photo booth mug shots at the mall. Adulthood separated us. Then we had to arrange times to be together and at those times, we discovered new revelations about our family ties. We refreshed our friendship, listened to one another, and encouraged each other.

There was a weekend trip to Port Townsend, Washington in 1989, soon after Beverly got her new job as a 911 police dispatcher. The job ended her financial worries and allowed her to visit more often. I drove while Beverly talked nonstop. Set free on our own, there was so much to say. Her

March Reruns

new job was fascinating and rewarding. She told me about the shock of realizing that several of the young officers had been born the year she graduated from high school! She enjoyed the role of mentor and listener.

Then there was the subject of our parents, fraught with issues only my sisters could truly understand. Beverly and I unloaded our memories on that trip, both good and bad. Our mother was in life limbo in a hospital bed. We marveled at how Mom first survived five years, beyond all expectations. Then ten years passed. We stopped being anxious and amazed and somehow assimilated the tragedy into a corner of our lives marked "Grief." Mom's condition had become so much a part of our lives that we accepted it as status quo. People stopped asking about her. People forgot. But we did not. I told Beverly that our church's new minister had met me and asked about my parents. I gave him the short version of the situation and he expressed his shock and sorrow. Ten years later, he left the congregation without ever asking me directly about her again. He was a talented, faithful theologian who unfortunately had no answers for me.

Nurses who cared for Mom had become family friends and they kept track of all of us. They created a wall of photographs, updated with each new grandchild and family milestone. Brenda was the most regular visitor and raised her daughters under the watchful eyes and interest of my mother's caregivers. My own grief intensified whenever another baby was born. Mom's final grandchild was the gift of our unexpected baby, Kirk. How I wished Mom could see him! Know him!

On that trip to Port Townsend, Beverly and I checked into a Victorian hotel complete with brass bed and claw-foot bathtub. Beverly was charmed. In a corner of the room, we found a trunk and opened it. Among the contents was a binder, a guest book of sorts, with an invitation to record impressions of our visit. Beverly set to work, creating the first two lines of a poem. I offered a line and we giggled, so impressed by each other's cleverness. Later that night, when the hotel was quiet, we sneaked out of our room wearing our bathrobes and crept down the stairs to the landing where an antique parlor organ sat against the wall. Beverly sat on the organ bench and posed for me, arms high, hands poised to strike the keyboard, like the Phantom of the Opera. Her eyes widened like Gloria Swanson in the final scene of *Sunset Boulevard*. We spit laughter, trying not to attract the attention of any other guests or the management.

When we settled ourselves in a charming restaurant, depending on our mood, talk might turn seriously to the subject of Dad, his failing health, and his future. Or we might get silly and compare notes on dining with Dad in a sort of "Can You Top This?" mode.

March Reruns

Brenda, Bev, and I shared this frustration. It had become the bane of our existence to try to entertain our father at a restaurant. First of all, he had to charm our servers. He could never just let them do their job and be direct and polite. He had to tease and engage them in conversation. As his tablemates, we were forced to listen to this, smiling all the while, but feeling annoyed. The happy occasion of being together somehow took a back seat to the stranger serving our table and the unhappy details of the menu at hand. Is the iced tea homemade? Dad's southern roots could not allow him to abide the powdered mixes that came from dispensers. This question usually startled the young waiter or waitress whose limited life experience allowed them to conclude that, yes, if the tea came from a drink dispenser, then yes, it was homemade. Dad could always tell the difference and the meal became a disappointment for something as simple as the lack of fresh iced tea.

My personal pique was a form of jealousy. I was rarely with him and I wanted his attention. I also wanted to please him. The law of chance turned against us at these occasions and I could usually trust that the delicious bread or menu specialty I bragged about was not available that particular day. He could not read the menu without his glasses, but he never remembered to bring them. The tirade about the forgotten glasses preceded the reading of the menu. As I read the

The Full Ripened Grain

menu to him, he would stare at other people around us, commenting and not listening.

"Isn't she a beaut?"

"Who?"

"That woman over there. My Gawd, those pants look like she was melted and poured into them."

"They make fantastic deli sandwiches here."

"I don't care for sandwiches."

I remembered that I served him a thick sandwich for lunch the previous day.

"Fine."

"Did you know Lucille Ball never sees her children? They neglect her terribly and she spends most of her time playing backgammon all alone."

"Really? How do you know this?"

"I read it in the *National Inquirer*."

"They have great New England clam chowder here."

"That sounds GOOOD. I'll have that."

"We only have red chowder today," said the waitress. "Manhattan style."

Beverly and I got serious about Dad's heart disease, which had continued to worsen since bypass surgery in 1980. His angina was often mistaken for a heart attack. He was nervous and a devoted Fred kept him company after work, making sure that emergency phone numbers were by the phone. After twenty-two years together, I knew Fred reassured Dad, and absorbed most of the fear and irritability my father produced. If not for Fred, they would have come our way.

March Reruns

I could not love Fred, but he loved my Dad. And for that reason it seemed the only decent thing to do was to meet him halfway and be civil. I tried to be kind and struggled with acceptance. Beverly did too. We heard each other. Fred annoyed Beverly with his "picky" nature. She invited them for homemade soup and bread and Fred brought along a piece of round steak, assuming Beverly would cook it for him. Soup wasn't enough for him. "I hope you don't mind," Dad apologized. She did mind. It was conflict that might have happened with any step-parent, no matter the gender.

Brenda and Beverly had their hands full with their jobs and busy families. Dad let us know we were "his life" and it was a heavy burden to carry. He was often depressed. According to Beverly, I didn't know how lucky I was to live so far away from everyone. Dad struggled daily to get by once his heart condition placed him on disability. He was friendly with his neighbors when working outside. He kept Fred's flower beds tidy and blooming with roses. He had no financial interest in the place and paid rent to Fred as well as his half of the utilities. His other friends were at work or gone, leaving his days filled with television, mostly. There were times he seemed desperate for contact and became angry and agitated when one of his daughters wasn't home to answer the phone when he called. His open schedule made time for lots of unexpected visits from him and it became a problem. Arriving unannounced, he acted hurt and

The Full Ripened Grain

disappointed if Brenda and Beverly had appointments or obligations. Brenda was building a business with her husband and was under constant pressure at the office. She told me that her stress was punctuated by frequent calls from Dad, just wanting to talk. If his calls didn't arrive in the middle of work, they interrupted dinner. They felt as if their lives were under constant surveillance. He cruised by their houses to see if they were home and noted whose car was in the driveway. He reported in when he thought a granddaughter was home alone, inappropriately, with a boyfriend. He was dumbfounded when his reports were unappreciated.

When Beverly asked Dad, tactfully, to please give her a call before coming by, he would drive the thirty minutes from his home, then stop at the phone booth near the corner of Beverly's house and say, "Hi, I was just driving by."

When calling me, his first question was always "When are you coming down?"

The pressure was uncomfortable, especially when accompanied by the need to see Mom. Wasn't once or twice a year enough? Travel was expensive. I longed to spend precious vacation dollars and days seeing other parts of the world. I tried to be truthful but I was vague and non-committal. He sulked. Dad made it hard to be truthful with him.

I shared with Beverly the two big lies I told our father. Once, when I was eight, a family conflict erupted. Dad's temper boiled over while trying to lay down the rules to Brenda, who was a defiant and emotional thirteen.

"Your own daughters are afraid of you!" she shouted.

I was struck dumb by an accusation that was too true to ever be mentioned aloud. He never came home drunk and smelly or high on drugs. But he could gripe viciously and rant and curse in his discontent. His round face was fair and glowed like an electric burner when he was mad. He spanked when we misbehaved, but he never beat us. I believed there was a difference. Later, as he sat solemnly at the kitchen table, he looked at me as I walked in.

"Is it true? Are you afraid of me?"

"No," I said, and embraced him.

When it was my turn to be thirteen, my best friend Kandy invited me to go to the beach for a whole week. We would be the guests of her Uncle John, a bachelor, who lived in a stylish apartment just blocks from the Pacific Ocean. Kandy's parents were nice people and trusted this man. Mom thought it sounded like fun and gave her consent. Dad balked. He was suspicious and his protective instinct was in high gear. He did not know Kandy's uncle and would not trust him to take care of me. His objection was understandable. We were pretty thirteen-year-olds, naïve and fully developed. I thought quickly and told him Kandy's grandmother would be there with us. Although

The Full Ripened Grain

Dad had never met her, it seemed like a good angle to try. It was a perfect lie, delivered perfectly. He bought it because I had never given him reason to doubt me.

Oh, the freedom! Kandy and I strolled the hot sidewalks, she in her first two-piece gingham bathing suit and I in my modest and matronly black one-piece. Kandy said it made me look "mature." Our hair was straight and long, like *Seventeen* cover girls. The Beach Boys' "Surfin' Safari" blasted from our new transistor radios. Kandy's Uncle John was wonderful! He even set us up with friends! They were two handsome brothers, sons of his close friends and neighbors. They were old enough to drive and close to college age. They took us swimming in their apartment pool and ice skating at an indoor rink where we held hands. They were fun and sweet to us. Kandy and I developed crushes on them in one day. At the end of the week, we listened to the English duo, Chad and Jeremy, sing on the radio "And when the rain beats against my window pane, I'll think of summer days again, and dream of you."

Later, Kandy learned Uncle John had asked them to "babysit" us. It was humiliating.

The week was perfect. But my treachery was tested one day when Dad called to see how things were going. He asked if Kandy's grandmother was there. I told him she had gone to the market and quickly added a true story I thought he would find interesting to divert him from the grandmother questions. Earlier that day, Uncle John's phone rang and I answered it. The voice on the other end, asking for John, was unmistakably familiar.

"Monty?" I asked. "This is Benay."

"Benay?" he said. "Have I called the wrong number?"

Monty was one of my father's bachelor friends who had visited our home several times. His deep voice with the Spanish accent chuckled with amusement when I told him I was a guest there. We both agreed it was a very small world. When Dad heard this, I could hear, but not understand why, the tension left my father's voice. Years later, I realized Monty had the dark good looks my father seemed to favor. Any friend of Monty's was a friend of his. I protected my lie. And so did Dad.

*Accept one another, then, just as Christ
accepted you, in order to bring praise to God.*

– *Romans 15:7*

THE TUNA REBELLION

When it comes to food, my husband is easy to please. For all of our life together, I have known Lynn's favorite simple meal is a tuna salad sandwich and tomato soup. For over thirty years, this food could elicit as much satisfaction from him as Thanksgiving dinner.

Then came that inexplicable moment when he announced that he did not care for chopped celery in tuna salad.

"What?" I said.

"I don't like the crunchy celery. I just want tuna and mayonnaise."

"Just tuna and mayonnaise?"

"Just tuna and mayonnaise."

"But what about the chopped dill pickle and the chopped boiled egg?"

"Just tuna and mayonnaise."

The Tuna Rebellion

His words landed like a slap on my face. I almost had to hold on to the kitchen chair to steady myself. My teenager, Kirk, sat in his chair at the table, stunned. A puzzled look passed between us. He was as confused as I. Kirk loved my tuna salad and said so, with the kind of sincerity a mother remembers.

After thirty years, the truth hovered in the room like…well, like stinky tuna. It was an incident that became etched in my mind as "The Tuna Rebellion." I believe it was his way of saying, "Don't take me for granted" or "You don't always have to have things made your way" or "Don't think you know everything about me." Had he been suffering in silence for thirty years, or did he suddenly change his taste? Was it that his mother once used only tuna and mayonnaise for his unsophisticated toddler palate? He told me his mother would ask him what he wanted for his birthday dinner and sometimes he would ask for tuna sandwiches and tomato soup. He could have had anything and he asked for canned tuna. Lucky mother. I would have asked for filet mignon.

Now that I think of it, he is a little too easy to please. He doesn't have a demanding bone in his body. Some people call it Norwegian Charisma. It is what Vice President Walter "Fritz" Mondale possessed. Reporters talked about it when he ran for the presidency of the United States in 1984. He lost big. American voters don't value Norwegian Charisma because it isn't flashy and dynamic. It is

The Full Ripened Grain

synonymous with caring and reliability. It is a trait brought about by strong women who instill strong character in their children. I think Walter Mondale's mother had a lot in common with my mother-in-law.

My husband's mother, June, died recently at age 86. She gave birth to him, nurtured his good character, and taught him faith in God. Together with his father, they set an example of devotion to one another, to their church, and to their community. Lynn shares these values with our children and me every day. My life has been better than it would have been because of him and, of course, because of her.

June's funeral was touching, with friends at her Lutheran church recalling her gifts of leadership. She was respected and admired. She was smart. As much as she was able to accomplish in life, I believe she suffered a lack of professional fulfillment borne by brilliant women of her generation. Being academically gifted as a teen in the 1930s meant she faced an uphill battle for education. The Great Depression uprooted her Minnesota family and money was tight. As a gifted mathematician, she wanted to go into science and medicine but gender and tradition forged her path. Marriage at eighteen and motherhood at nineteen put her professional dreams on hold. Her husband's work took precedence over hers. When the time was right, however, she worked as an

The Tuna Rebellion

accountant. Later she opened her own retail business.

I have lived a married life not so different from hers. But I grabbed the educational opportunities open to me by the 1960s and postponed marriage a little longer than she did. I had access to safe birth control, delaying parenthood until nearly thirty. And I did this with her best work at my side—her son. Knowing my attachment to my own children, I realize now how hard it must have been for her to see him married so young. His new college diploma was hardly dry when we set out on the road to a new life in another state. She would follow, but not until years later.

I have heard it said that men choose to marry women who are a lot like their mothers, while women look for their fathers in their mates. I have also heard it said that we look for qualities in our spouses that were missing in our parent of the opposite sex. Both are good theories.

I considered myself nothing like my mother-in-law, except for our ample bust line. She and I did not laugh at the same humor. While a television comedian had me howling, my mother-in-law would sit silently, making me feel embarrassed for having understood the off-color humor. She enjoyed music, but could not sing. I sing a lot. June liked violets and pansies, the delicate flowers. I like bright bold floral colors—the marigolds, the geraniums, and the tough stuff like rhodies. She could not eat spicy food because of a food allergy.

I adore spicy food and felt inhibited trying to cook for her. She did not drive. I could not live without the freedom of driving a car. She was not a shopper and felt no pressure to dress or decorate her home in the latest fashion. She had sales resistance and was frugal until the last. Comparatively, I am a spendthrift and a clothes horse. I just like to go shopping once in a while. She seemed to have trouble "playing" and usually put up verbal roadblocks to what might be considered "goofing off." I'm willing to put chores aside for a day if it is for something more appealing—like sharing time together.

But when it came to parenting, we taught the same important values of faith, honesty, personal responsibility, education, and empathy for others. She usually handled all home responsibility when the demands of her husband's job kept him distracted. I expected Lynn to keep up his end of the bargain as best he could, given the parameters of his career obligations. I traveled some in my volunteer work for higher education and trusted Lynn to be a good caregiver. My mother-in-law usually stepped in as well, understanding my need to take part in the community outside my house and making it possible for me to participate when the children were small. She was a trusted ally. Despite our different temperament and tastes, we loved the same people and that was reason enough to get along.

The Tuna Rebellion

My mother-in-law's Scandinavian reserve was not stern, but polite and loving. It made her harder to understand, but it made my husband easier to understand because of the intimacy marriage provides to get past that reserve. If I can adjust to those attributes in my husband which are unlike anyone in my own gregarious family, I can also allow myself to finally accept and appreciate qualities shared by my husband and father.

In Lynn, I found the missing pieces of my father, but I didn't know it until now. When we married, I would have argued loud and long that he was nothing like my father. Lynn was smart and ambitious and spoke about plans for his future career. He wanted an education as much as his parents wanted it for him. He was politically aware, even at age eighteen. Okay, so he did happen to be 5 feet 11 inches tall, the same as my dad. So they both had brown hair and brown eyes. They really did not look the same at all. And temperament? Night and day. Dad's quick temper and fastidiousness about his appearance was nothing like my easy-going husband. And mostly, Lynn liked guy things, like watching basketball and football. He loved military history and aviation. He built scale models of airplanes and cars. He likes cars. My dad liked cars. Hmmm.

As a musician, my father did his work at night. It left him time to keep house for himself and his partner. His house was polished, clean as a whistle. He enjoyed his garden and he proudly showed me his rosebushes in bloom. He planned meals and shopped for groceries. He was also the one present at home when contractors remodeled and service people arrived and left. His partner was away at his job and came home to some domestic order. I do the same thing, but society gives me its full support despite the fact my father was a better gardener and housekeeper.

Lynn is very nurturing to me and our children. My dad changed diapers as much as my mother, I am told. Dad was a good cook, a musical man and very funny when he wanted to be. Lynn's Scandinavian reserve gives way to a thoroughly skilled sense of humor when he allows people to get close. He too is a music lover, a solid choir baritone. On a weekend morning, he will often be the cook. He makes a better omelette than I do. And I never worry that he will starve if I don't make it home for a meal. He is thoroughly capable of helping himself. His mom taught him how to mop a kitchen floor, wash dishes, and do a load of laundry. My father did the same things. We have taught our children how to do homemaking chores, knowing that sharing these tasks is really more about sharing a loving home, respect and teamwork than the issue of masculine or feminine. With some maturity on my part, I have come to see and appreciate the qualities shared by my husband and the father I distanced with a thousand miles of mixed feelings.

*God is able to make all grace abound to you,
so that in all things at all times, having all that
you need, you will abound in every good work.*

– 2 Corinthians 9:8

CHANGES

The 2009 Best Actor Oscar went to Sean Penn for his portrayal of Harvey Milk, the first openly gay man elected to office in San Francisco. It is a film that would have been impossible to make under the Hays Code moral criteria that dominated the entertainment industry for most of my father's lifetime and much of mine. The *Seattle Times* recently printed a photograph of Washington's legislative contingent of openly gay representatives. They smiled on the steps of the capitol, a legacy of pride and dignity started by Mr. Milk. But the legislative debate over insurance coverage for live-in partners still makes headlines. The moral debate incites us to learn more. We remain curious but resistant to change. The final change will come when it is not relevant to acknowledge gay or straight politicians.

Watching Hollywood or government change is threatening enough to some, but not nearly as threatening as life in our own small sphere. In my own life I see love and acceptance of same-sex relationships among friends whose children have found it easier to come out to their generation. I recently watched the baptism of an infant whose godparents were her uncle and his adored partner. It was a joyful event, divine in both spiritual and worldly grace. I expect there were some in the congregation who didn't approve and felt awkward. Change is hard. Tradition and culture are strong. Mores are weak. They battle one another, exposing crevasses in society that are too deep and too wide for many to cross.

I watched the film *Brokeback Mountain* twice to absorb the dialog and wonder anew at this tale of an adulterous—yet tender—love story between two men. The film begins in 1963, about the time of my parents' first separation. By the end of the story, which spans twenty years, the character Ennis has a 19-year-old daughter who visits her father to tell him she is engaged and would like him to attend the wedding. Ennis is alone in his poorly furnished trailer. He is a divorced, financially unsuccessful father, still loved by his daughter, who comes to him with this big news in her life. The whole scene felt very familiar.

I had a somewhat similar experience in 1971 when I tentatively approached my father's small apartment to tell him I wanted to be married. Like the daughter in *Brokeback Mountain*, I did not bring my fiancé with me. I expected Dad would

Changes

not love the idea and wanted to spare Lynn, who had always been respectful but quiet around my father. Dad resented the time and attention I gave to him. I knew Dad found it hard to accept my growing up and actually felt sorry for him as I knocked on his door to deliver a message that felt like betrayal.

I was nervous and glad to find him alone.

"Dad, Lynn has asked me to marry him and I said yes."

"Oh...Honey," he said and leaned his face into the palm of his hand.

"We would like to get married this summer," I said, ignoring his anguish.

"But what about college?" he asked.

"I have every intention of finishing college next year. I will just be a married student."

He lightened up surprisingly quickly.

"My parents were married on June 24. Maybe you could pick that day."

He seemed reassured, although his interest in my education was dubious. He never paid for any of it. Whenever Dad asked about my classes, I would start to explain what they were and what I was studying. There was a polite pause while I began to tell him, but he usually interrupted me, not quite interested enough for any detail.

"I can never remember what you are studying," he said. "Someone asked me the other night, and I couldn't remember that word."

The Full Ripened Grain

"Communications," I said, feeling mildly disgusted. "Writing, journalism, advertising." On a February night a month later, he picked me up to take me to dinner at a cafe. I knew he didn't have much money. He didn't have a job at the time and only had a couple weeks of unemployment left. I didn't know what to do for him.

My student loans paid tuition and I had a part-time job as a night receptionist in a car dealership. Mom always came through with some cash for spending at the end of a home weekend. But in three years of college, Dad had given me only two checks for twenty-five dollars each. That night I gave him fifty dollars. We were even. I did not broach the subject of wedding costs. Neither did he.

As hard as it might have been for Dad to accept changes in me, he also found it very hard to accept changes in our mother, his ex-wife. She became the first woman to serve as the president of the West Covina Chamber of Commerce in 1970, a time when bras were being burned to call attention to the women's movement. Newscasts all over the country began to feature women on-camera, reporting women's entry into formerly male-dominated professions.

It wasn't only Dad who did not quite recognize our mother, transformed. Arriving at her dress shop on a weekend back from college, I might find her standing near her desk with her ear attached to the phone. Instead of the usual affectionate greeting, she would tap her fingers on the newspaper lying on the counter, pointing out yet another article that mentioned her name. There was a photo of her with then-Governor Ronald Reagan, signing a bill the Chamber endorsed. My mom was standing there in the photo with the guy we California college students resented for his conservatism and insults. Today I look at the photo and think how amazing it is—my mom with the man who became President of the United States.

I was unnerved by this change in my mother's status and selfishly withheld a lot of praise for her efforts. I acted like a resentful five-year-old whose mother keeps talking to a friend, ignoring me tugging at her skirts. She made sure I was invited to special dinners for the business community. I thought she was "showing off" but now I realize she was trying to show me positive change and possibilities.

I sat in the audience at her installation as president and she was proud to introduce me. I felt proud too, until her acceptance speech included the quotation of the entire text of the poem "Desiderata." It was an inspirational poem which was new to her. But in my developing and not fully-educated mind, it was an unoriginal and embarrassing cliché. Among us "worldly" college students the poem was plastered all over our dorm walls on posters stylishly enhanced with an aged, weathered look. We all bought the posters, thinking it was wisdom from the 17th century (which seemed more profound than wisdom of the current age or our parents' age). In fact, it had been written about 1920, the year my dad was born, by Max Ehrmann, a lawyer from Terre Haute, Indiana.

I thought, couldn't she just say her own words? Completely lost on me was the sheer will, the drive and the courage this woman had shown going into the limelight to make a mark on her local community. Mom had three and a half years of high school, no diploma, and it was her secret. I think it was a secret she guarded more rigorously than the fact her gay husband had divorced her. How I wish I could apologize for my arrogance.

Mom was smarter and more talented than she knew. She only approached her potential because she was a naïve Southern girl with inadequate education, caught up in the role expected of women of her generation. She had a great deal of natural savvy and a good sense of humor, so she did well in retail management. I wonder now why she never went back to school. She needed encouragement from all of us, but I regret we failed her by just expecting her to get on home from work and feed us and take care of us. How I wish I could do that part over.

Mom was an optimist, a hand-picked antidote to our father's depression and pessimism, thank God. I think being married to Dad, the "Gripe King," made her try harder to encourage us. What better thing can be said of a mother but that she loved us unconditionally, found pride in us, trained

Changes

us how to put our best foot forward, and never criticized. I thank God she did as well as she did despite the fact her life was not that easy. Brenda, Beverly, and I were able to love others and be successful human beings because of the basic love and good care she gave us as children. People ask me how I turned out so normal and managed to raise happy, ambitious children. It is because I was loved and have learned to love God, even though my parents suffered human flaws as I do.

Their divorce did some damage, to be sure, but all the basics were already there to help us get through it. It was to Mom's credit that she did not waste a lot of time with a bitter attitude. She made the most of her new life before she became a sleeping beauty. I now realize the long vigil became twenty years of her spiritual presence in my life. God used this waiting period to foster my understanding of patience, love, anger, fear, resentment, greed, and grief.

Dad. Daddy. His was a crippling struggle against his nature, and a society that denied him dignity and acceptance as a normal and creative human being. His struggle became our struggle and left us all with fearful secrecy and estrangement from one another and a loving, forgiving God.

Overweight and stressed, Dad developed type 2 diabetes at age fifty. By age sixty, in 1980, he had severe heart disease, no doubt aggravated by years in smoky nightclubs. He had bypass surgery and needed care to get through recovery. I flew south

The Full Ripened Grain

to spend a week with him. I was thirty by then, a mother and not working full time. My sisters needed some support so I attended Dad while his partner, Fred, was at work. He explained that he shared a house with Fred for economic reasons. They shared costs as roommates and the subject of any other attachment wasn't mentioned. Dad put my things in "his" bedroom, but slipped up later by telling Fred to place something in "our" bedroom. Struggling for health, my father persevered with a charade he was desperate to continue for my sake. Tragically, I never found the courage to relieve his pain and help him tell me his story.

One night, getting into the guest bed across the hall, a thought occurred to me. I returned briefly to Dad's room and quickly tucked him in as he had done for me as a child.

"I love you, Dad."

"I love you, too."

Once I was home, my husband helped me contact his godfather, a minister named Pastor Joe Luthro, who coincidentally lived near Dad. Pastor Joe agreed to visit my father, who welcomed him. I do not know how many times he visited or what they talked about. All I know is that Lynn's faith and the faith of this pastor gave my father the opportunity for personal peace. He lived another dozen years with health problems and irritations of daily life, but when he sat at the piano, he always started playing "He Touched Me," a song about being lifted of burdens and being made whole. I

Changes

am reassured that God did his best to give him the acceptance and compassion he needed.

I thought my father had left me nothing. I was wrong. What he left me was the means to the greatest compassion I will ever know; a means to love and acceptance that makes me a truer, freer human being and one closer to God. Because of what He helped me through, I have a life here on earth that is closest to the one He has in store for me when I leave it.

"Never be afraid to trust an unknown future to a known God."

– Corrie ten Boom

AN ANNIVERSARY IN MAY

Mother's Day 2006 brings back the pain that lasted twenty years, during which my family and I waited as my mother spent her life from age 49 to 69 in a persistent vegetative state (PVS). She was a victim of horrific medical malpractice in a Southern California hospital. I missed her then and I miss her now.

The petite and energetic mother we loved and respected left our lives in May, 1976, thirty years ago this week. My sisters and I were in our twenties when the tragedy happened. Afterward, there were no letters, no phone calls, no joys shared, no burdens lightened with her wisdom and experience. We watched and waited, bearing her grandchildren and growing to middle age as she lay in limbo. I was only twenty when I wrote in my journal: "Mom would tell me, 'Don't be afraid to speak up and say what you know.' Mom knows a

An Anniversary in May

lot more than I give her credit for." Now that clever insight makes me smile a little.

How I needed her!

News of the Terri Schiavo case and the interference of the U.S. Congress this past year made me recoil. The media angered me for printing, again and again, the photo of Terri with her eyes open and her teeth showing, as if she were ready to converse. It was a false impression, giving momentum to the national outcry against the court's decision to allow her long-waiting husband to withdraw an unnatural impediment to natural death—a feeding tube.

Early on in Mom's medical crisis, we "pulled the plug" in agreement with our stepfather. But my mother lived and breathed on her own. Then the bitter disagreements set in as her husband prepared a malpractice suit in order to sustain her treatment. The cost was already past a million dollars by 1977. He authorized six major surgeries to keep Mom alive despite every indication she had catastrophic brain damage. My sisters and I argued that it was cruel to put her through these procedures. We felt strongly that our mother would not have wanted to have her life sustained by extraordinary means. But there was no living will, no statement of her preferences. We had no legal standing compared to my new stepfather, who had married my mother eighteen months prior. The woman who gave birth to us, whose history was linked forever with ours, was outside our legal

The Full Ripened Grain

influence. We never filed a court injunction to stop it. We were young and naïve, with few resources for the vast legal fees we would have to pay to challenge my stepfather's decisions. I felt powerless and also felt pressure to return to my job and husband back in Washington State after being absent for weeks. I needed to work. We could have sold our modest homes and everything we owned and not made a dent in the cost of our mother's medical and legal bills. And then, there was the chance each operation would end her life, mercifully.

She lived. The doctors could restore her body, but not her brain. The hindbrain, the section of the brain that controls the things we do automatically—such as breathing, heartbeat, and digestion—survived.

The situation was hideous. The first years of treatment left her subject to every kind of infection. A yeast infection damaged her eyes. She was almost blind then, dying piece by piece. Each intestinal infection, the results of peritonitis, could have ended her life. Five months after the first surgery, she was ashen, balding and skeletal, her chest heaving. There was wakefulness and sleep. There was no awareness, no communication. But her husband was giving the orders. Still the doctors operated, afraid of lawsuits for refusing treatment. Legal briefs were beginning to pile up in the courts as my stepfather sued every entity connected to the hospital and the equipment used to treat my

An Anniversary in May

mother. When her case came to court in 1980, the evidence of negligence was overwhelming. An out-of-court settlement provided funds for my mother's care. My sisters and I decided to cooperate and signed away our right to sue for wrongful death when the time came. It was her husband's legal right and responsibility to see that the funds were used to provide that care and he did, hiring around-the-clock nursing care and maintaining clean, beautiful surroundings for her in a private home. A court-appointed officer scrutinized the spending and there were legal reports to file. A legal trust was established by 1987.

A tracheotomy left a permanent hole in Mom's throat. When she could no longer take nourishment by mouth, the nurses gave her water and food through a feeding tube. These skilled women kept her skin in healthy condition and manipulated her body to keep her from having bedsores. The attending doctor visited every three months and marveled at my mother's stamina and the nurses' excellent care. He kept up those visits for all twenty years.

Mom was moved to a new suburban house in Los Alamitos. She continued to get the care she deserved—private care in a pretty yellow and cream-colored bedroom. Brenda kept a weekly vigil, spending her precious day off work to bring her children to pay respect to our mother. She forged a strong relationship with the caregivers. Beverly came often, then less frequently, and chose

The Full Ripened Grain

not to take her children with her to visit the sad-looking lady they did not know. My visits required a plane trip once or twice a year for the two decades she lived in that condition. As they were born, pictures of her grandchildren lined the walls, the little faces smiling and maturing with the years. Mom's face changed little. Away from direct sunlight and stress, her face stayed placid, her skin unwrinkled.

Caregivers aged and were replaced, but there were two nurses who stayed with my mother, one for fifteen years and the other for eighteen. I was so grateful to them! These women were surrogate eyes for my mother, watching her daughters' lives play out with characters and events she could not know. They grieved with us when our father died of heart disease in 1992 and Beverly died in 1993. But mother lived on. It made no sense at all to me.

How many times did people ask me: "Is she in a coma? Can she hear you? Can she communicate with you in any way?" Their well-meaning questions left me feeling drained every time I tried to explain her existence. No, I told them, there is no comprehension. Every birthday, every Christmas, every Mother's Day, my tears fell while reading Hallmark cards to send. Gifts were lotions, music, nightgowns, flowers, anything I could think of that she might smell or feel or hear. But year in and year out, in guilt and torment, I prayed that God would release her soul from this limbo and take her home. He took His time answering.

An Anniversary in May

If it had been up to me to decide, would I have withdrawn the feeding tube and ended my mother's life? The answer might have changed if I had been asked at different intervals along the journey of her life and mine. Is five years long enough to wait? Ten? Fifteen? I don't know the answer, but nobody asked me. Frankly, I was damned angry at God about it and damned tired of feeling guilty for wanting it to be over.

Thirty years ago, I watched my mother take communion in our Lutheran church the week before the tragic "routine" operation. I couldn't remember seeing her do this before, kneeling at an altar. She had faith even though she didn't talk about it much. Knowing that, and knowing the hope in Jesus Christ it inspires, would I have withdrawn artificial means to keep her alive and released her spirit?

But God had other plans for her and for me. It isn't surprising to me that Terri Schiavo lived thirteen days past the withdrawal of food and water. Any person who could have sustained fifteen years in a bedridden state has an amazing physical constitution. But when it comes to spiritual matters, who can underestimate the will of an individual to survive? Even with severe brain damage, what is it inside us, as human beings, that can resist the cessation of heartbeat, breathing lungs, kidney function? Recently, a young woman driving an SUV plunged six stories off a bridge into Oregon's cold Willamette River. She survived

The Full Ripened Grain

the impact, arms and legs intact, able to swim for her life. In a separate incident, a party overdose of alcohol took the life of a young woman. We have no idea, really, what our bodies can handle.

My mother's endurance and our long vigil both baffle and inspire me. The experience was like taking the same plunge into the dark river with that woman and coming up breathing, fighting to continue life despite the pain and fear.

We human beings are at once delicate and intricate and temporal like the tulips in an April field and sturdy, resilient, and enduring as Mt. Rainier when the will inspires us. We are individual miracles, those who live in vegetative states and those who wait with them.

*We always hope; and in all things it is better to hope than
to despair. When we return to real trust in God, there will no longer be room in our soul for fear.*

– Johann Wolfgang von Goethe

GHOSTS OF SNOWATER

We were away from home on a major kid holiday. It was the clearest indicator of our almost-empty nest. Two days before Halloween, I should have been filling candy bowls, searching for old costumes, digging out decorations from the cluttered garage, and carving a pumpkin for the front porch. But this year, our timeshare at Mt. Baker, near the U.S.–British Columbia border, was available October 29. We decided to go.

We expected our youngest son, a high school senior, to accompany us and perhaps bring a friend. However, the prospect of having no parents around for a whole weekend was infinitely more appealing to him than a drive in the autumn landscape of northern rural Washington State. We coaxed him half-heartedly but did not insist he come with us. Our feelings were conflicted, knowing that a weekend vacation at Snowater timeshare, with no kids, could be a whole new adventure. We arranged for our boy to stay with a buddy and his parents, which made him happier than we would have preferred. Sadly, we noted, it just wasn't very long ago that he loved going to this place with us.

We drove north in our cozy VW Jetta instead of the family van. We glided up the familiar meandering two-lane highway, little changed in twenty years, past black and white Holsteins in foggy pastures, past Victorian bed and breakfast inns advertising VACANCY, past silver silos and graying barns, past yellow aspen leaves banked by winds against fence posts, past Christmas tree farms planted with fir seedlings and abandoned overgrown firs, past the produce stand with APPLES painted across the roof, past the shaded forest ranger station, until we saw Snowater. As we turned into the driveway, memories hovered over us like mist in the evergreens.

Snowater became our "cabin in the woods" in 1985. It was a place to be with each other, with our children, and with no other distractions. We had access to it four weeks a year, which was good news for people with lots of vacation time and not enough money to fly anywhere. The one hundred

Ghosts of Snowater

and fifty mile drive delivered us from small-town obligations to glorious isolation.

On those weekends, there was no dwelling on my mother's sad condition. But on quiet solitary hikes by the river, I missed her. I thought of her in her bed, far away. Her life was so unfair compared to my freedom to walk and communicate with those I loved. I prayed and asked God to be with her and in her and to reach the soul we could no longer see in her eyes. I believe with all my heart that He did this. By the time her tragic life ended, I had regained a great deal of emotional strength to accept it. I had not yet realized the source of that strength was from her and God, who made her my mother.

There was quiet time to think about Dad, too, and how I might bridge that difficult communication gap. My father's private life with his partner endured for twenty-five years, longer than many legal marriages. I did not love his mate, as many find it hard to love a stepparent. I could not fathom their passion and devotion for each other any more than Dad could fully appreciate the private passion and devotion between my husband and me. Their daily life did not involve me or my immature embarrassment. That became a minor detail in his life of parenting, work and struggle for self-acceptance. He visited us in (mostly) good humor and was proud of us and our lives. It shames me to admit I never graciously invited Dad's partner to visit us. I told myself he chose to stay

The Full Ripened Grain

home. I came to accept that I was not responsible for Dad's anger or those cruel years we struggled as a family. God chose him to be my father. He was a worthy human being for whom Christ died. And when Dad died, it was God, not self-righteous hatemongers who judged him. He is loved and forgiven as I am.

Toward the end of her life, Beverly was our guest at Snowater and relaxed with us. There was a tough road ahead of us we could not foresee. For the time being she was on call as the children's funny, affectionate aunt. We were blessed with enough time for them to remember her, always.

In retrospect, that time at Snowater provided an occasional weekend inventory of my blessed marriage and family. Over the years, we stuffed our minivan full of some forbidden foods and toys, books, skis or roller skates, depending on the season. When we retired the baby car seat and play equipment got bigger, we added a cargo shell on the roof filled with snowboards. On the way we sang, listened to story tapes, and always stopped, at least once, to eat at a favorite coffee shop. When our children hit adolescence, personal CD players kept squabbles to a minimum.

There was poor television reception at Snowater, which meant entertaining the kids with our own ingenuity. When it rained and the evenings were long and quiet, their father relaxed and became an unself-conscious comedian, reading children's books aloud. His voice changed with the characters, taking on various accents. The kids surrounded him, cuddled on the sofa bed. They adored it and laughed so hard, mainly at their dad when tears streamed down his cheeks from chuckling. The older they got, the more interesting the books became. A new game, Trivial Pursuit, arrived and we could play in teams with our baby boy getting answers whispered in his ear for him to say out loud.

At first, all three kids were small enough to sleep together in the large sofa bed. We pulled rank and kept the one bedroom to ourselves. Then we brought sleeping bags for the floor. The kids never seemed too cold or too hot and slept well after a long day of fresh air. We woke to their giggles in the morning.

There was a well-equipped kitchen, perfect camping for a city girl who never learned to cook outdoors. Somehow, exchanging our roomy house for a 500-square-foot condo wasn't a problem. We owned all the outdoors and the Nooksack River banks. As time passed, the kids got old enough to play with less supervision, giving us a few peaceful moments to be alone.

But who is kidding whom? As one friend said about the cozy timeshare, she had to do everything she usually did at home for her three small children, except with less room and less equipment. What was fun about that? The roaring Nooksack was dangerous. We had to be vigilant.

The Full Ripened Grain

There were small feuds between husband and wife over who got to play and who had to watch the kids. Getting a family in and out of a swimming pool or wet ski clothes is tiring and creates piles of laundry. Who wants to deal with the grief of a five-year-old who isn't allowed in the hot tub? Who likes being hounded to go swimming at 6 a.m.? And with no television, there were no Saturday morning cartoons to give a parent an extra hour of sleep. It was togetherness All Day Long—All Weekend. In hindsight, by the time we got home, we were, frankly, relieved. And now we wouldn't trade that time for anything.

For the Halloween weekend by ourselves, we packed lighter than ever. We relished the drive with no complaints from the rear. We listened to "our" music. We waited until we reached Bellingham to go to a grocery store where we chose gourmet treats and wine. We ate pumpkin pie for breakfast because we could. The only thing we cooked was coffee, sipped late in the morning, in bed, with our favorite books and each other. We smiled a lot, gleefully.

No event and no place can ever really stay the same, because we change. Leaving Snowater that weekend, I left behind some of the nostalgia and sadness that life transitions can bring about. Together, we explored the historical Fairhaven district in Bellingham, so quaint with brilliant maple leaves covering the sidewalk as we strolled. We took the slower, scenic Chuckanut Drive southward, marveling at this northwest horizon we had never seen before in thirty years of living in Washington State. We were in a new place with a new view.

We made it home by dark. After all, there was still a pumpkin to be carved.

The End

ACKNOWLEDGEMENTS

I want to express my appreciation to dear friends, like Adele Cornils, who thought my family's experience should be made into a book. And thanks to those who had faith that I could write and tell our story. I am indebted to the Field's End Writer's Community on Bainbridge Island, Washington and to each of my instructors, who nurtured my skills and educated me about the book business. Thanks to my editor, Jim Whiting, for his wise advice and patience.

My love and thanks go to my Octopus pals, high school girlfriends who lived this firsthand, who allowed me to read to them at reunions, and who accepted me and cheered me on to this day. To my Enumclaw Koinonia Church Circle, whose young faith nurtured my own and helped me to face life's crises. Thanks too, to the Last Friday Book Club. I give thanks for your friendship, shared wisdom, and willingness to read the first draft. Much appreciation goes to the individuals who read my manuscript and gave me feedback.

Special thanks to Dr. Randall Riggs, MD, who listened to me and helped me.

And finally, thanks to my husband and my extended family for their love and support.